Shanghai

Text by J.D. Brown
Photography by Shen Kai
Cover photograph by Bill Wassman
Design: Roger Williams
Series Editor: Tony Halliday

Berlitz® POCKET GUIDE

Shanghai

First Edition (2006)
Reprinted 2008

PHOTOGRAPHY CREDITS
All pictures by Shen Kai, except: pages 1, 2B, 12, 29, 74, 75, 80 by Bill Wassman; page 15 by TopFoto; pages 16, 17, 18 by Roger Viollet/ TopFoto; page 21 by TopFoto/ImageWorks Cover picture by Bill Wassman

CONTACTING THE EDITORS
Every effort has been made to provide accurate information in this publication, but changes are inevitable. The publisher cannot be responsible for any resulting loss, inconvenience or injury. We would appreciate it if readers would call our attention to any errors or outdated information by contacting Berlitz Publishing, PO Box 7910, London SE1 1WE, England.
Fax: (44) 20 7403 0290;
e-mail: berlitz@apaguide.co.uk
www.berlitzpublishing.com

Nanjing Road Pedestrian Mall is a golden mile of upmarket department stores and shops (page 32)

The Shanghai Museum tops the list of China's very finest displays of historical treasures (page 34)

The Oriental Pearl TV Tower affords a birds-eye view of the the 'new' Shanghai (page 64)

TOP TEN ATTRACTIONS

Dongtai Lu Antiques Market is the place to go for collectibles and souvenirs (page 43)

The 16th-century Yu Garden (page 37) is one of China's best-preserved classical gardens

The Bund is an outdoor museum of grand colonial architecture, while the Bund Promenade is the city's prime people-watching post (page 25)

Ancient Suzhou (page 73) is criss-crossed by picturesque canals and studded with classical Chinese gardens

Soong Qing-ling has a huge following, at both her former residence (page 56) and her mausoleum (page 60)

Shanghai's acrobats perform nightly in several of the city's theatres (page 89)

Longhua Temple is the city's most vibrant Buddhist centre (page 59)

CONTENTS

A ➤ in the text denotes a highly recommended sight

Fact Sheets

INTRODUCTION

In a single decade Shanghai has transformed itself from a gritty, dilapidated metropolis into a trendy, modern megacity, festooned with Starbucks and skyscrapers. At first glance it hardly seems a Chinese city at all. As legions of steel, concrete and glass poured across Shanghai's cityscape in the mid-1990s, Shanghai ruthlessly redrew itself into the richest, trendiest, most modern destination in the People's Republic of China (PRC), and it is now setting its sights on becoming the most important city in all of Asia.

Yet Shanghai's transformation is hardly complete. The city remains a massive work in progress, and its rough edges are never entirely out of view. Around the corner from the latest fast-food joint or designer-label boutique lies the local bird and flower market, its wares pitched in the street, blocking traffic. Above the six-lane superhighway cutting through the heart of the city, a blind beggar strums

> Local wisdom holds that Shanghai men are calculating, reserved and ambitious to achieve a high-quality lifestyle.

his *erhu* on the pedestrian flyover. An older Shanghai frequently surfaces, its ways and fragrances completely unfamiliar to those more used to the modern cities of the West.

Even the old Shanghai was in significant measure Western, or more precisely, colonial. For almost 100 years, from the 1840s to the 1940s, Shanghai was a colonial outpost, presided over by British, French, German, American and even Persian businessmen. No other city on mainland China was so international for so long a period. The Western legacy is still stamped onto the heart of the city, from the old French Concession with

The Nanjing Lu

its mansions, boulevards and terrace houses to the 'architectural museum' of monumental banks, trading houses and private clubs forming the legendary Bund along the waterfront.

While Shanghai is buoyant about its future, brassy about its new wealth and increasingly international in its outlook, it has not shed its Chinese character or entirely cast off a sense of its past. This is a city that has always valued commerce and consumption, style and status, money and power, but it also knows something of beauty and joy, so it should not come as a surprise to learn that mainland China's best museum, its most interesting residential architecture and its most vibrant entertainment scene are also contained in Shanghai. Thanks to a modern metro system, masses of new taxis and the surprising compactness of the city's main sights, Shanghai is a city that one can explore close up, on foot. It is a city of neighbourhoods old and new that reward urban rambles.

Chinese women doing morning exercise in the Shanghai Stadium

Population

The sheer mass of people in the streets is an inescapable aspect of Shanghai. No one knows the city's exact population, which is always increasing with the daily arrival of peasants drawn by Shanghai's promise of un-

> More than two-thirds of Shanghai's office workers, citing worry about work, the hectic pace of life and after-hours entertainment of clients, report sleeping no more than six hours a night.

told riches, but the census takers have paused for the moment at a figure of over 16 million, with some 7 million in the main urban districts. That does not take into account the 3 million registered migrant workers or the 6 million undocumented workers from the countryside. The community of temporary foreign residents is minuscule by comparison, pegged at about 80,000, but when combined with the arrival of several million foreign tourists yearly, the Western influence on businesses, restaurants and bars is considerable. By 2015, Shanghai's official population could reach 23.4 million, according to United Nations estimates.

Shanghai's citizens are overwhelmingly Han Chinese, with most residents from the city or nearby towns. The Shanghainese speak their own dialect, although the Beijing version, known as *putonghua* or Mandarin, is standard across China. English is the most widely spoken foreign language, but few residents use it.

Shanghai now has its own millionaires – indeed, its own billionaires – along with a growing middle class and a sprinkling of beggars.

Climate

Shanghai can be miserably hot in July and August and icily cold by January. Rain reaches its peak in the spring. The most pleasant month to visit is usually October, when the

> The rise in global temperatures, combined with Shanghai's slow sinking into the soft delta, has led experts to forecast a rise in sea level here of 1cm (nearly ½ inch) every year.

summer cools down and the typhoon season ends, followed by April and May, when days are mild, if a bit soggy. To avoid hordes of tourists, however, one might risk travel in March or November. Year round, Shanghai is one of the more polluted cities in the world, with poor air quality, limited visibility and streamers of smog plastered to the horizon.

A City Under Construction

Unlike many cities in China, Shanghai does not have a long history nor is it rife with ancient temples and pagodas, although its Yuyuan Garden and nearby teahouse rank among China's finest. Rather, what sets Shanghai apart is its extensive collection of colonial architecture dating from the late 19th and early 20th centuries, when British traders and other colonialists took up residence by force. These resident outsiders built the European-style mansions, apartments, gardens and boulevards that continue to impart a romantic air to Shanghai.

After China's liberation by the Communist Party in 1949, the colonial legacy of Shanghai suffered first from neglect, then, with the unleashing of free-market economics in the mid-1990s, from the threat of sheer progress. Shanghai woke up with a jolt, bulldozers and lifting cranes tore through the city and double-digit economic growth became a way of life. Shanghai's commercial acumen let little stand in its way, and Shanghai's historic city-centre neighbourhoods started to come down piece by piece.

Concurrently, on the east side of the Huangpu River, directly across from the moribund buildings of the Bund, a new Shanghai was built from scratch. Known as Pudong, the new city quickly became home to the world's highest hotel, Asia's largest department store and China's biggest stock exchange. Pudong was unequivocally the Shanghai of the future. For the first time an old and a new Shanghai stared across the river at each other, the staid and crumbling Bund on one shore, storm-trooping skyscrapers on the other.

China's City of the Future

As the 21st century began, even old Shanghai gained a new look, acquiring rafts of its own high-rises. The city put up over 10,000 new high-rise buildings in a little over 10 years, and not all of them were in Pudong. Fortunately, many of Shanghai's colonial mansions, traditional stone-gate houses, Buddhist temples and age-old street markets were not obliterated, and the Bund was largely untouched, although it was being

The emerging skyline

dwarfed by walls of glass and steel rising high over its back. At this point, Shanghai seemed to discover a use for its past that was compatible with its reawakened commercial spirit. The old buildings that survived were renovated and leased to upmarket developers, serving as anything from apartments to cafés. Boulevards were redecorated in period lampposts and cobbled walks. Nineteen-twenties apartments were converted into designer-name boutiques. Mansions became European restaurants or bars serving Guinness on tap.

The Chinese legacy of Shanghai, with its classic gardens and shop houses, has likewise undergone commercial conversion, the city's version of historic preservation, resulting in pedestrian-only shopping and eating complexes such as the Old Town Bazaar and Xintiandi. Even the buildings lining the Bund, their ageing interiors off-limits to visitors for decades, are now opening their doors to visitors for the first time in many decades, thanks to investments by swanky international shops and trend-setting restaurants.

A face of Shanghai

Today's visitor can find both Shanghais, old and new, amply represented, although it is the new Shanghai, embodying the new China, that has the momentum. Past, present or future, Shanghai has always been a city of commerce.

A BRIEF HISTORY

The story of Shanghai is marked by three great transformations from its original incarnation as a fishing settlement: first to trading capital, then to Communist city, and most recently to modern world city. Each of these turning points recast the city's architecture and its economic role, and each reflected Shanghai's underlying commercial character.

Fishing Village to Market Town

The first great change in Shanghai's development came as the small fishing settlements dotting the Yangzi River delta coalesced into a market town. During the Tang Dynasty (AD618–907) the settlement occupying what is today central Shanghai was known as Hudu. It was located on the ocean, which explains the name it later acquired, Shanghai, meaning 'above the sea'. Hudu's fishing enterprises dwindled as great dykes were constructed across the delta, pushing the original coastline further east out to sea. By 1292, Hudu had been transformed from a fishing village into a trading centre, the chief market town in a prosperous county known as Shanghai.

By the 16th century, the heart of Shanghai County was a walled city 5km (3 miles) in circumference, encircling the present-day Old Town area (Nanshi). Its population had by then reached 200,000. In 1732, an Imperial decree made Shanghai the regional headquarters for collecting customs and tariffs. Utilising its site on

As Asia's wealthiest, most cosmopolitan and cultured city, with the finest shops and restaurants, Shanghai in the 1920s became known as the 'Paris of the East'. At the same time dance halls, brothels and opium dens gave it the name of 'The Whore of Asia'.

Suzhou Creek and the Huangpu River, with access to the East China Sea and the mouth of the Yangzi, Shanghai now became the primary port of entry and exit for China's ocean-going trade. The city was primed for a change from market town to seaport, just as Western business interests were arriving in force.

Opium, Silk and Taipans

A major metamorphosis, exploiting Shanghai's position as an ocean-going port, began in the 1840s when colonial powers from the West, primarily Britain, occupied and rebuilt much of the city, making it China's trading capital. The Lord Amherst Expedition, scouting sites for the East India Company to set up shop in China, made an initial foray up the Huangpu River, reaching Shanghai in 1832 and bringing opium into the country. The First Opium War (1839–42) followed, as did a fleet of British warships, trying to protect their country's opium trade. In June 1842 the British command took up residence in Yuyuan Garden and dictated terms.

They carved out a concession in central Shanghai where they could live beyond the reach of any Chinese authority. The French followed in 1849, and the Americans established their Shanghai settlement in 1854. In 1863 the Americans and British consolidated their Shanghai claims as the International Settlement, but the French Concession in western Shanghai remained French. Both foreign districts maintained their own governments, courts, schools, utilities, police forces, voluntary armies, public works and tax collectors.

Opium was widely used in the West: Sherlock Holmes used to visit the Chinese opium dens of Limehouse, east London, and in 1875 San Francisco passed the first anti-drug law in the US, aimed at the Chinese opium dens.

Shanghai harbour in 1875

Shanghai became a Western colony, in fact if not in name. The Shanghai Chinese were not pleased, and resistance first came to a head in 1854 at the Battle of Muddy Flat, where a few hundred British and American volunteers turned back a few thousand Imperial troops, and later in 1860 and 1862, when Taiping rebels, hoping to overthrow China's Qing Dynasty, were driven from Shanghai in large part by foreign militia.

Meanwhile, the foreign merchants settled down to make money. Soon in control of the tea, silk and opium trade, the richest foreigners, known as taipans, began to rebuild their settlements in Shanghai along Western lines. Although the foreign population of Shanghai by 1860 was little more than 500, its influence was far-reaching. Nanjing Road, their main shopping street, was extended from the Bund westwards to the new racetrack; Christian churches, schools and hospitals were established throughout the city; and Captain George

Shanghai women in a wheelbarrow

Balfour, the first British consul, undertook the reconstruction and embankment of the riverfront, laying the groundwork for the Bund, which rapidly became the centre for shipping and trade. Shanghai was destined to become more international in look and character than any other major city in mainland China.

Both of the city's foreign districts expanded greatly. The International Settlement, administering its holdings through the Shanghai Municipal Council, controlled 190 hectares (470 acres) when it was formed in 1863. By 1900, it encompassed 21,500 hectares (53,000 acres) of today's central Shanghai. The French Concession, with its avenues and mansions, eventually covered 10,000 hectares (25,000 acres) of prime urban real estate.

China's Wealthiest City

Colonial Shanghai's greatest period of growth occurred in the early 20th century. Most of the monumental edifices along the Bund date from 1910 to 1930, a period when the population of the city doubled to nearly 3 million and more than 800 new factories appeared. Banks from around the world located branches on the Bund, from which they dominated Chinese financial affairs after the fall of the last Imperial dynasty, the Qing, in 1913. Foreign shipping companies moved in, funded by such British enterprises as Jardine Matheson and Swire, powerful foreign companies known as hongs. In the 1920s, steamship companies began taking tourists up the Yangzi River from Shanghai. Foreign oil companies set up petroleum storage yards on mudflats on the east side of the Huangpu River. By 1924, Shanghai had become one of the world's busiest shipping ports, handling half of China's foreign trade, and it was soon producing nearly half of all China's tax revenue, collected in the Shanghai Custom House, which still stands on the Bund.

A class of Chinese entrepreneurs, parallelling the colonial taipans, was also created in Shanghai, along with a Chinese version of the mafia, known as Triads. In early 20th-century Shanghai the Triads presided over the gambling spots, opium dens and houses of prostitution that lent to the city the notorious image for which it was known worldwide.

At the same time that Shanghai was enjoying its status as China's wealthiest city, revolutionary movements were being nurtured. Major protests against foreign influence over

A Western tourist, around 1900

A Japanese tank on the streets in the Sino-Japanese war

Chinese affairs broke out several times, notably in the student-led May 4th Movement of 1919 and the labour strikes issuing from the May 30 Incident of 1925. Within the liberal confines of the French Concession, the Chinese Communist Party was born in Shanghai in 1921, with Mao Zedong in attendance. The Communists held their annual congresses there, before being brutally removed from the city by forces, including the Triads, favouring Chiang Kai-shek's central government.

Japanese Invasion

Despite political conflicts, Shanghai's foreign concessions prospered, even after Japanese warships docked at Shanghai's harbour in 1932, rather as British warships had some 90 years earlier. Japan launched a second attack on Shanghai five years later, defeating Chiang Kai-shek's Nationalist forces. A gradual process of military occupation ensued, and by 1943 the Japanese had full administrative control of Shanghai. Of Shanghai's 60,000 foreigners, most of those who did not flee the Japanese occupation ended up in local concentration camps, a harsh fate dramatised in J.G. Ballard's *Empire of the Sun* and a film version of that novel by Steven Spielberg.

The Japanese were expelled at the end of World War II, when Allied forces, led by the US, briefly occupied Shanghai in 1945. In the civil war that soon engulfed China, the Communists prevailed, their Red Army liberating Shanghai in 1949. The city was finally in Chinese hands, but those who had fuelled its economy, foreign and Chinese businessmen alike, were gone, as were those who had given Shanghai its colour for a century, from criminal gang leaders and sing-song girls to refugee rabbis and Jesuit priests.

A People's Shanghai

Under Chinese Communist rule, Shanghai lost its market economy and cosmopolitan feel, but it also lost its 500 brothels, its gambling dens, its drug dealers and its other outlets of vice and corruption. The gap between rich and poor was immensely narrowed. Foreign businesses were nationalised. By 1961, just two dozen foreigners were left in Shanghai. Along with the rest of China, Shanghai cut itself off from most of the world, including its once-helpful Communist ally, the Soviet Union.

The Communist victory ended Shanghai's colonial period, but it hardly altered the city's appearance. Shanghai became something of a decaying time capsule. The Bund gained new Chinese tenants, Nanjing Road's department stores became state-run, and churches and mansions were converted into factories, schools and crowded apartments. Nor did Shanghai change dramatically in the 1960s or 1970s. Chairman Mao, struggling to reassert his leadership, slipped into Shanghai in 1965 where his wife, a local actress named Jiang Qing, controlled the print media, and launched what is now known as the Cultural Revolution (1966–76). Mao directed his young Red Guard followers to raze all remnants of traditional Chinese culture and Western capitalism. In Shanghai the Red Guards tore down Confucian temples, looted Buddhist and Daoist shrines, used cathedrals for storage and destroyed foreign graveyards. They also persecuted thousands of Shanghai citizens, particularly those with any connections to Westerners, as documented in such memoirs as Nien Cheng's *Life and Death in Shanghai*.

Shanghai only returned to its commercial ways in the 1980s, after the death of Chairman Mao, as free-market policies flowered and foreign investment started to flow in.

Shanghai Rebuilt

China's new reformist leader, Deng Xiaoping, vowed in 1992 to build Shanghai into a world-class economic centre

Build a Better Toilet

Shanghai's redevelopment extends to even the humblest of structures. With a legacy of on-the-nose public toilets, the city in 2005 hosted the World Toilet Expo and Forum as part of an effort to make unhygienic lavatories history. Central Shanghai now has a public restroom every 300m (1,000ft), with signs mapping the nearest location of a WC. A new generation of public toilets falls under a five-star rating system based on features such as Western-style toilets (as opposed to squat models), toilet paper, soap, running water and automatic flushing. The city's officials appear to agree with the World Toilet Foundation's Jack Sims, who told the Shanghai forum, 'Our happiness cannot be complete without a proper and pleasant toilet environment.'

as rapidly as possible, spurring what has become the most rapid transformation in the history of the city. Within five years, Shanghai was operating far more construction cranes than any other city on earth. Weekly the skyline was altered, and daily the city rose from its ashes. The rate of progress was almost incomprehensible. A whole new city was constructed from scratch on the east side of the river in the Pudong New Area. Within 10 years Shanghai again ranked as one of the world's five busiest ports, a position it had last held in colonial times.

A man sits on his demolished house in Old Shanghai

At first Shanghai's unbridled development took a severe toll on Shanghai's classic neighbourhoods, distinctive architecture and cultural treasures, but more recently Shanghai has formulated a commercial solution to preserving its past. To house its artistic and archaeological treasures, Shanghai has built China's finest museum. To resurrect its religious traditions, it has rebuilt Daoist and Buddhist temples reduced to ruins during the Cultural Revolution. To save what remains of its rapidly disappearing old neighbourhoods, Shanghai has allowed foreign residents to purchase restored villas, upmarket restaurants to refurbish French Concession mansions, international boutiques to line restored avenues and foreign consortiums to turn stone-gate residences into glitzy shopping malls. The most famous shopping street in China, Nanjing Road, has been revived by banning cars and opening the avenue to pedestrians.

Shanghai's latest urban renewal project, also connected with preserving its colonial past, focuses on the Bund. By encouraging upmarket international retailers and restaurateurs to turn former banks and office buildings into shopping galleries, Shanghai has finally begun to reopen the biggest doors to its architectural past. The North Bund Development Plan now underway will extend the Bund revival northwards across Suzhou Creek, where apartments, a luxury hotel, seven office pavilions, themed courtyards and an extension of the pedestrian promenade along the Huangpu River are in the works.

The future is bright: a baby-crawling contest

The North Bund project is just one of many riverside developments that the city has slated as it gears up to host the officially sanctioned Shanghai World Expo in 2010. The Expo should serve as the city's coming-out party. After a century seething under colonial rule, followed by some painful decades in Mao's shadow, however, Shanghai is already showing itself off.

Historical Landmarks

4000BC Fishing villages occupy Shanghai-area marshes.

AD618-907 Shanghai known as Hudu village during Tang Dynasty.

1292 Shanghai becomes lower Yangzi delta's chief market town.

1553 City wall built around today's Old Town (Nanshi).

1559 Construction of Yuyuan Garden begins.

1732 Shanghai opens customs house for foreign trade.

1784 Huxinting Teahouse used as cotton cloth brokerage hall.

1842 British settle in Shanghai after First Opium War.

1854 Shanghai Municipal Council governs foreign concessions.

1863 British and American settlements join to form International Settlement; French Concession remains separate.

1895 Japanese establish factories in Shanghai.

1912 City wall surrounding Old Town is demolished.

1921 Chinese Communist Party formed in Shanghai.

1928 Greyhound racetrack opens in French Concession.

1929 Cathay Hotel (Peace Hotel) built by Victor Sassoon.

1936 China's most famous modern writer Lu Xun dies in Shanghai.

1937–45 Shanghai occupied by Japanese forces.

1945 Japanese expelled; US troops arrive.

1949 Communists take over; Chen Yi becomes Shanghai mayor.

1952 People's Park and People's Square occupy old racetrack.

1966 Cultural Revolution isolates and impoverishes Shanghai.

1972 Shanghai Communiqué restores US–China relations.

1982 Hongqiao Development Zone accepts first foreign investments.

1990 China's first stock exchange opens; Pudong airport begun.

1994 Metro Line 1, China's second underground railway, inaugurated.

1995 Pearl of the Orient TV Tower becomes symbol of new Shanghai.

1997 Ex-Shanghai mayor Jiang Zemin takes over as China's leader.

1999 Pudong International Airport receives first flight.

2004 Shanghai stages first Formula One Grand Prix in China.

2005 Mayor Han Zheng announces 14 consecutive years of double-digit growth in the city.

WHERE TO GO

Despite its immense population, Shanghai is a city that can be seen largely on foot, thanks to the compact layout of its main neighbourhoods. The transport system (primarily taxis and the Metro lines) is inexpensive, efficient and easy to use, bringing even the most remote urban attractions within a 20-minute journey of the city centre.

HUANGPU (CENTRAL SHANGHAI)

The heart of old Shanghai is the Bund, a showcase of monumental colonial-era architecture flanked by a wide pedestrian promenade along the shores of the Huangpu River, Shanghai's avenue of trade and shipping. Immediately west of the Bund is another colonial legacy that has undergone modernisation, Nanjing Road, now a pedestrian shopping mall until it reaches Renmin Park and Renmin Square, where several of Shanghai's most important cultural treasures lie. The whole central-city area, from the Bund to Renmin Square, extends about 2km (1¼ miles), with two Metro stations along the way.

The Bund

Old Shanghai's riverside was a muddy bank when British colonialists arrived after the Opium War of 1842 and began to develop it as China's leading port for the tea and opium trade. The wall of Western banks and trading centres that now lines the river dates from the height of the colonial era, the 1920s and 1930s, when Shanghai was known worldwide for its wealth and libertine lifestyle.

> **The name 'Bund' comes from an Anglo-Indian word meaning an embankment on a muddy shore.**

Landmarks along the Bund

▶ **The Bund** runs 1.6km (1 mile) from the Waibaidu Bridge
(1906) on Suzhou Creek south along present-day Zhongshan
Dong Yi Lu, taking in a score of historic buildings with
addresses in numerical order. Until recently the interiors of
nearly every building were closed to visitors, either abandoned or consigned to government use, but over the past few
years building after building has been restored, many for
commercial or tourist use, and by 2010, when Shanghai
hosts a World Exposition, the Bund, including massive new
developments, will be the hottest spot in the city. Already the
colonial structures are being dwarfed by modern towers rising to the west, and across the river the skyscrapers of
Pudong are casting a long shadow on this architectural museum of days gone by.

At the north end of the Bund, its oldest building (1873), the
former British Consulate (Nos 33–53 Zhongshan Dong Yi
Lu), was razed in 2004 as part of an urban renewal plan. The

seat of British power in China for a century, this complex of bungalows later served as Shanghai's first Friendship Store. The next two buildings along the Bund – the Banque de L'Indo-Chine (No. 29), built by French interests in 1911, and the Glen Line Building (No. 28), erected in 1922 – are occupied by the Everbright Bank. Next door is the former Jardine Matheson Building (No. 27), opened in 1927 as the headquarters for one of Shanghai's pre-eminent foreign trading houses. It is currently the Shanghai Foreign Trade Building.

Beside it, the former Yangtze Insurance Building (No. 26), built in 1916, is occupied by the Agricultural Bank of China, which has restored its lobby. Next door (No. 25) is yet another bank, starting in 1924 as the Yokohama Specie Bank and continuing today as the Industrial & Commercial Bank of China. The last building on this long block has not changed owners, but it, too, is a bank, a 1937 Art Deco behemoth, the Bank of China, with a grand lobby from the late colonial period.

Just around the corner, with its entrance at the start of Nanjing Road (No. 20), is one of the Bund's true sightseeing gems. Now known as the **Peace Hotel**, it was opened in 1929 as the Cathay Hotel by Shanghai's most celebrated

Extensive – and Expensive

With 14 million people (depending on how you count), and with a metropolitan area covering about 6,000 sq km (more than 2,300 sq miles) – four times the size of London – Shanghai is one of the biggest cities in the world. Administered as a separate region, like Beijing, the Shanghai metropolis includes rich farmland as well as big-city housing complexes and heavy industry. Shanghai is not only extensive but expensive. A recent cost-of-living survey ranked it as the sixth most expensive city in the world, ahead of such notoriously expensive cities as London, Geneva and New York.

The Peace Hotel was where Noel Coward holed up to write *Private Lives* and where Steven Spielberg filmed scenes for *Empire of the Sun*.

taipan, Victor Sassoon, a Jewish investor from Baghdad. It retains its spectacular Art Deco interiors, including a labyrinthine lobby, a gilded ballroom (8th floor), the ornate Dragon Phoenix restaurant (8th floor) and a rooftop garden (11th floor; admission fee) under the massive green pyramid dome – still the signature of old Shanghai.

Across the street (No. 19) is an even older hotel, built in 1906 by the Sassoon family as the Palace Hotel. Its marble lobby and main restaurant also reward viewing, as they too remain little changed. The next building south of Nanjing Road (No. 18) is the former Chartered Bank of India, Australia and China. Built in 1923, it has recently been renovated into an upmarket shopping and restaurant tower, called Bund 18. The North China Daily News Building next door (No. 17), now the AIA assurance company building, was home to China's oldest English-language daily newspaper after it opened in 1921, and neither it nor the final building on this block, the 1924 Bank of Taiwan Building (No. 16), have been opened to visitors.

The next two buildings – the former Russo-Chinese Bank Building (No. 15), built in 1901, and the former Bank of Communications Building (No. 14), built in 1940 – continue the financial theme that the Bund exemplified for most of its history, as both are still financial institutions. Their immediate neighbour to the south has more historical merit. The **Shanghai Customs House** (No. 13) was the pre-eminent trading institution in Shanghai when it opened under its bell tower (known here as 'Big Ching') in 1927, but today its dark lobby only hints at its former grandeur. Far more startling is the foyer of the next building, the former Hong Kong and Shanghai Bank (No. 12), the present-day **Shanghai Pudong Development Bank**, its columns laid and wooden lobby first polished in 1923. Just inside the revolving doors is a magnificent panelled dome depicting eight of the world's great financial capitals, from London to Shanghai. The second-floor Bonomi Café provides espressos for those who want to linger over the interiors.

The next block contains four more buildings, three of which are not yet developed or open to the public. The fourth, today another bank but formerly the headquarters of the Nishin Navigation Company (No. 5), is the home of Shanghai's first world-class international restaurant, **M on the Bund**, perched on the seventh floor of this 1925 edifice. On the last block to the south, the former Union Insurance Company Building (No. 3) is now known as Three on the Bund, a smart commercial restoration that kicked off the

Dome of the Shanghai Pudong Development Bank

modern resurrection of the colonial strip. Its swanky remodelling immediately attracted chef Jean Georges Vongerichten, clothier Giorgio Armani and the Evian Spa.

The Bund's last two buildings to the south have places in colonial history, but not in a sightseer's itinerary. The Shanghai Club (No. 2), built in 1910, was the old boys' private club for decades, but it is presently boarded up, its legendary Long Bar long gone; and the McBain Building (No. 1), once the Asiatic Petroleum Building, is after nine decades home to the China Pacific Insurance Company.

The Bund Promenade

Paralleling the Bund of banking is a Bund for strolling. The **Bund Promenade** is a walker's paradise, hugging the shore of the busy Huangpu River and presenting panoramic views of old Shanghai immediately west and new Shanghai on the eastern shore. Nearly everyone who comes to Shanghai walks the length of this embankment. River cruises depart almost hourly from the docks on its southern end.

Toward the northern end, near the statue of Shanghai's first Communist mayor, Chen Yi, a comrade of Chairman Mao on

---

The Old Signal Tower

At the southern end of the Bund Promenade stands an odd piece of history – the **Signal Tower** (1 Zhongshan Er Lu), a brick spiral 49m (161ft) high that was built in 1865, and rebuilt in 1884 and 1907, to transmit weather reports and time measurements by a system of flags and signals to ships in the river. In 1993 it was moved about 20m (65ft) to its present position at the foot of the Promenade. The Signal Tower keeps changing uses these days; sometimes it's a bar or café, sometimes a museum with old photographs and sometimes even a lookout again, its spiral stairway open to visitors.

the Long March, is the entrance shaft to the **Bund Sight-Seeing Tunnel** (open Mon–Thu 8am–10pm, Fri–Sun 8am–10.30pm; admission fee), a quick way for pedestrians to reach the other side of the river aboard a subterranean tram with its own light show. Here too are the remains of tiny Huangpu Park (daylight hours; free), the former British Public Gardens (1868), notorious for supposedly posting a sign reading NO DOGS OR CHINESE ALLOWED. Most Chinese were not allowed in the park until 1926.

Monument to the People's Heroes

Above the park is a granite obelisk erected in 1993, the **Monument to the People's Heroes**. Its basement houses the **Bund History Museum** (1 Zhongshan Dong Yi Lu; open daily 9am–4pm; free), its curved walls lined with photographs of the Bund's colonial days and displays of rare artefacts such as flags, boundary markers and settlement documents.

Nanjing Road

China's most famous shopping street, **Nanjing Road**, is divided between Nanjing Dong Lu, which begins at the Bund next to the Peace Hotel and runs west to Renmin Park, and Nanjing Xi Lu, which continues west past Shanghai Centre and Jing An Temple. Shops – small and large, old and new – line the entire 4km (2½ miles).

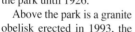

Deliveries outside the No. 1 Department Store

Some of the most interesting stores and landmark colonial structures are situated along the **Nanjing Road Pedestrian Mall** (Nanjing Dong Lu from Xizang Zhong Lu east to Henan Zhong Lu). French-designed and opened in 1999, the mall attracts as many strollers as the Bund Promenade, mostly window-shoppers. Few of the shops are traditional; most are modern and international. An electric sightseeing trolley (which you pay for) serves as a shuttle for foot-weary visitors.

From the Bund it is a crowded two-block walk to the pedestrian mall, where there's plenty of room to spread out. Much of Nanjing Road has been altered by the construction of new shopping arcades and towering complexes, such as Century Square, but Shanghai's original 'Big Four' department stores, dating from the 1920s and 1930s, are still in service. The former Wing On Department Store (at No. 635 Nanjing Dong Lu) is now the Hualian Commercial Building, and the former Sincere Department Store (No. 650) is now a fashion store, while the former Sun Sun Department Store (No. 700) occupies its 1926 building as the Shanghai No. 1 Provisions Store. The largest of them all, The Sun, now the No. 1 Department Store (No. 800), still packs in over 100,000 shoppers a day, thanks partly to an ultra-modern 22-storey annexe.

Renmin Park

In colonial times, **Renmin (People's) Park** (231 Nanjing Xi Lu) was part of the Shanghai Racetrack (1863). It opened as central Shanghai's largest public park in 1951, and is popular with families and retired people doing *tai chi* exercises in the morning and playing *mah-jongg* in the afternoon. Fronting the park's entrance on Nanjing Road are the 1933 **Grand Theatre** (216 Nanjing Xi Lu), still screening American movies, and the **Park Hotel** (170 Nanjing Xi Lu), one of the world's tallest buildings when it opened in 1934 and still worth a look inside for its austere Art Deco features.

On the east side of the park, along Xizang Zhong Lu, is a reminder of the future – **Raffles City**, a brand-new mega-mall – and the past – the **Moore Church** (316 Xizang Zhong Lu), the first church to reopen in Shanghai (1979) after the Cultural Revolution. South down Xizang Zhong Lu is another historic building, **Great World** (1 Xizang Nan Lu), built in 1915 and in its day a notorious centre of vice. In recent times it became a respectable emporium of family entertainment, including acrobatic and martial-arts performances, although there is some doubt it will dodge Shanghai's bulldozers much longer.

Shanghai Art Museum (325 Nanjing Xi Lu; <www.sh-artmuseum.org.cn>; open daily 9am–5pm; admission fee), on the northwest edge of Renmin Park, has occupied a 1933 neo-classical clock-tower building since 2000, following a careful

Shanghai Art Museum

Admission to Shanghai Museum, Shanghai Art Museum, Shanghai Urban Planning Exhibition Centre and Shanghai Grand Theatre – all on Renmin Square – can be bought at any of the sites' box offices. These money-saving tickets cover various combinations of the four attractions, but they are good for one day only.

restoration of its elegant marble interiors. The exhibition halls feature works by modern Chinese artists, and on the top (5th) floor is an American restaurant, Kathleen's 5, with a splendid view of the area.

Renmin Square

A southward continuation of Renmin Park, **Renmin (People's) Square**, at the intersection of Metro Line 1 and 2, is home not only to a new Shanghai City Hall, but to three of old Shanghai's modern showcases of culture.

The **Shanghai Museum** (201 Renmin Da Dao; <www.shanghaimuseum.net>; open Sun–Fri 9am–5pm, Sat 9am–8pm; admission fee) is the city's and China's finest gallery of traditional treasures. Its 11 galleries and three special exhibition halls encircle a four-storey atrium and use state-of-the-art lighted displays, with signs in English and Chinese. Arranged chronologically within each gallery's theme, the museum has particularly stunning collections of stone sculpture, antique bronzes, scroll paintings, coins and dynastic furniture. The museum bookshop has Shanghai's most complete selection of works in English about Shanghai and China. The courtyard outside the entrance is one of the city's premier kite-flying arenas.

The first floor contains galleries devoted to bronze works, some dating from the Shang Dynasty (1600–1100 BC), and ancient stone and clay sculptures, with an emphasis on Buddhist images. The second floor has a ceramics gallery with tricoloured figures from the Tang Dynasty (AD 618–907) and pottery from the Ming Dynasty (1368–1644). The third floor has a superb gallery of paintings on silk scrolls, a calligraphy display and a collection of carved seals (chops), the ink stamps used by emperors and officials to sign documents. The fourth floor contains galleries of jade work, coins and old furniture, as well as a display of minority costumes and artefacts. While the 120,000-piece collection is not the largest in China, it is the best displayed, and its arrangement of artefacts is remarkably concise.

The **Shanghai Urban Planning Exhibition Centre** (100 Renmin Da Dao; <www.supec.org>; open daily 9am–4pm; admission fee) is more interesting than it might appear at first blush. This building of the future addresses Shanghai's urban development, past and future, in detail, not solely by photographs or charts but by an immense scale model of Shanghai 2020 that engulfs the third floor, evoking the full

Calligraphy in Shanghai Museum

A girl about town in busy central Shanghai

dimensions of this monster city in a way that the view from the tallest observation tower cannot.

Also on Renmin Square is another cultural complex, the French-designed **Shanghai Grand Theatre** (300 Renmin Da Dao; tours daily 9–11am, 1–4pm; admission fee). It is a thoroughly modern (1998) glass structure with sweeping marble staircases, performance studios and three of Shanghai's plushest theatres.

NANSHI (OLD TOWN)

Shanghai's **Old Town** (Nanshi District), southwest of the lower Bund, encompasses the remains of the walled city where the Chinese lived and conducted business for centuries. It remained quite Chinese even during the colonial period (1842–1949), escaping the modernisation that affected much of central Shanghai. The city wall and moat disappeared for the most part in 1911. Today, the northern portion of Old Town has been redeveloped for the benefit of tourists, its narrow lanes and old Chinese houses and shops restored in 1991 to serve as the Yuyuan Bazaar, a pedestrian mall to rival that of Nanjing Road. Shopping is the byword here, and the mesh of lanes is almost always densely crowded. At the heart of the bazaar are an old teahouse with a zigzag bridge, a classical garden, an old city temple and a street of antiques shops and teahouses, all to be explored on foot.

Yu Garden (Yuyuan)

Yu Garden (open daily 8.30am–5pm; admission fee) was built by Pan Yunduan, a local official, between 1559 and 1577. It remains one of southern China's best-preserved private classical gardens. Encased in a streaming dragon wall, the layout is a 2-hectare (5-acre) maze of arched bridges, rockeries, goldfish ponds and dozens of Ming Dynasty pavilions. The entrance to the garden is on the north side of the teahouse pond in the heart of Yuyuan Bazaar. Just inside the main gate is the Grand Rockery (Dajiashan), a Ming Dynasty masterpiece of stone sculpture in the form of a mountain 14m (46ft) high. From the pavilion on top of this hill, the Ming official could watch all the excitements of river life, though tall buildings now intervene.

Ming Dynasty pavilion and goldfish pond in Yu Garden

At the front of the Hall of Ten Thousand Flowers grows a 400-year-old gingko tree. Another carefully created rockery is reflected in a pond teeming with giant goldfish.

All the corridors and pavilions, bridges and walls, sculptures and trees are so artfully arranged that the garden seems many times larger than its actual, compact size. There are gardens within gardens, each one attended by graceful pavilions, and most visitors quickly get lost, but there are exit signs at major intersections.

Among the highlights are the Three Ears of Corn Pavilion (Sansuitang), built in 1760 as a hall for merchants, its wooden beams and window frames carved with the emblems of the harvest. The Spring Pavilion (Dianchuntang) contains weapons and coins used by the Small Sword Society in the 1850s during an uprising linked to the Taiping Rebellion against China's ruling dynasty and the colonial powers in Shanghai. Other treasures in the garden include the Exquisite Jade Rock (Yulinglong), a monumental stone slab carved by the waters of nearby Lake Tai and owned by a Northern Song emperor in the 12th century, and the Inner Garden (Neiyuan), a world unto itself once reserved for women only.

Shanghai Old Street

The southern boundary of the Yuyuan Bazaar is **Fangbang Zhong Lu**, recently restored (2000) as Shanghai Old Street. When the city wall stood, a canal flowed here. The entrance gate is on the west side at Henan Nan Lu, where

---

Huxinting Teahouse

The most picturesque teahouse in China, **Huxinting Teahouse** (open daily 8.30am–10pm) stands just outside the Yu Garden walls, on the northwest shore of a goldfish pond crossed by the Bridge of Nine Turnings (its zigzags are intended to deflect the path of ghosts). Built in 1784, it served Shanghai's cloth merchants as a brokerage house, and did not become a teahouse until the late 19th century. The second storey of this black-eaved pavilion is ideal for a cup of Chinese tea. Be warned that the bridge can become the most congested overpass in the city by late morning.

Shanghai Old Street

an early Sunday morning antiques market is the draw. Stretching eastwards for 800m (½ mile), Old Street is packed with antiques and collectibles housed in traditionally styled shop houses. There are teahouses and jewellery shops along the way, too.

The main historical attraction is **Chenghuang Miao** or the Temple of the Town God (249 Fangbang Zhong Lu; open daily 8.30am–dusk; admission fee). It has been the city's main place of Daoist worship since the early 15th century, and is still an active shrine, dedicated to Shanghai's God of Commerce. Its open courtyard is often packed with worshippers.

Old City Wall

Purportedly the last remnant of Shanghai's ancient city wall is located directly west of the Yuyuan Bazaar on Dajing Lu at Renmin Lu. The **Ancient City Wall** (269 Dajing Lu; open daily 9am–4pm; admission fee) consists of a three-storey tower (the former Temple of the War God) with a few exhibits about life in Shanghai's Old Town and, attached to it, a section of the city wall, although locals say it was not part of the old city wall at all. The original brick wall dated from 1553 stood 8m (27ft) high and measured nearly 5km (3 miles) in circumference. This memorial section of the city wall is about 50m (160ft) long.

A block east of the city wall is the **White Cloud Daoist Temple** (Baiyunguan). It was moved from its original location at Xilinhou Lu in 2004 and reopened with its treasures intact, including rare Daoist scriptures from the Ming Dynasty and a row of seven gilded statues that are be-

seeched daily by supplicants with petitions ranging from long life to greater wealth.

Dajing Lu is perhaps the only actual remnant here of Shanghai's past, a piece of pre-Revolutionary Chinese life, its fragrant wet market blanketing the cobblestones every morning with fresh food and livestock. Like many of the old streets in Nanshi District, however, Dajing Lu is slated for the bulldozer (perchance to be restored itself one day, as Old Dajing Street).

Confucius Temple

In the southwest quarter of Old Town, Shanghai's **Confucius Temple** (Wenmiao) was restored and reopened in 1999 (215 Wenmiao Lu, east of Zhonghua Lu; open daily 9am–4.30pm; admission fee). The grounds, which are tranquil and seldom crowded, include a genuine Qing Dynasty pagoda, fresh statues to China's great scholar and such followers as Mencius (Mengzi), and galleries featuring unusual stones and teapots. A second-hand book fair is held in the courtyard on Sunday mornings. Another recently restored place of worship in Old Town is the **Xiaotaoyuan** or Peach Garden Mosque (52 Xiaotaoyuan Jie; open daily sunrise to sunset; free). It is Shanghai's main mosque (opened 1927), with a minaret and separate prayer halls for men and women.

A local man sitting by the Old City Wall

LUWAN (FRENCH CONCESSION)

Notable for its tree-lined boulevards, terrace-house villas and European-style buildings and mansions, Shanghai's French Concession has some romantic neighbourhoods in which to stroll. Beginning where Old Town (Nanshi) ends, at Xizang Nan Lu (the former boulevard de Montiguy), and running westwards along Jinling Zhong Lu and Yan An Zhong Lu (the former avenue Foch West), it is crossed by the modern shopping boulevard of Huaihai Zhong Lu (the former avenue Joffre). Metro Line 1 runs east–west beneath this street, making Huaihai Zhong Lu the main artery in every sense for getting around the French Concession.

Xintiandi

Two blocks south of the Huangpi Nan Metro stop and Huaihai Zhong Lu, down Madang Lu, is Shanghai's most upmaket restoration project to date, **Xintiandi** (<www.xintiandi.com>). The name means 'New Heaven and Earth', and for visitors hoping to find many of Shanghai's finest restaurants, bars and boutiques in one swanky pedestrian mall, it is divine. Opened in 2001, Xintiandi heralded the path that Shanghai has since followed to preserve its past, particularly its architectural legacy: that is, to restore and convert to high-end commercial purposes its ageing villas, mansions and traditional residences. In the case of Xintiandi, the converted blocks were occu-

> **Nearly 4,000 families lost their *shikumen* homes due to urban renewal in the Xintiandi/Taipingqiao project of 2001, including relatives of the world-famous architect I.M. Pei, whose 100-year-old childhood residence on Huang Pi Nan Lu was demolished despite his personal appeals to Chinese leaders.**

pied by fine examples of *shikumen* architecture, the stone-gated, two-storey lane houses that became Shanghai's most popular residences for Chinese tenants in the 1930s. In Xintiandi, these terrace houses were polished up and converted into two main blocks of shops, plazas and alfresco dining establishments, anchored by a Starbucks.

The urban development east of Xintiandi includes a large lake and park (Taiping qiao) surrounded by new office and residential towers. In the undeveloped fringes of this old neighbourhood is Shanghai's premier antiques

Dongtai Lu Antiques Market

and collectibles market, with scores of stalls and shops, the **Dongtai Lu Antiques Market** *(see page 84)*. *(see page 84)*

The old neighbourhood's inner life is preserved in the **Shikumen Open House Museum** (No. 25, Lane 181, North Block, Taicang Lu; open daily 10am–10pm; admission fee). Its two floors are decorated in the furniture and belongings of a typical *shikumen* resident of the 1920s.

On the east side of Xintiandi is another historic brick and marble building, the **Museum of the First National Congress of the Chinese Communist Party** (374 Huangpi Nan Lu; open daily 9am–4pm; admission fee), where the Chinese Communist Party was founded by Mao and others on 23 July 1921. When the French police learnt of the clandestine meeting, they raided the two-storey corner house. But they arrived too late to find Mao and the other 11 conspirators. The Communist founding fathers continued their congress aboard a hired excursion boat on a lake.

Fuxing Park

Branching off Huaihai Zhong Lu is a lane recently redeveloped as a colonial-style 'food street', **Yandang Lu**, which ends at the main entrance to Fuxing Park (open daily 6am–6pm; admission fee). Opened by colonial residents in 1909, and once known as French Park, it now contains a statue of Marx and Engels and is where locals practise *tai chi* and ballroom dancing amid the old plane trees and rose gardens.

At the northwest edge of Fuxing Park, Gaolan Lu is a nicely maintained French Concession lane, highlighted by the **Church of St Nicholas** (16 Gaolan Lu). This 1933 Russian Orthodox church with its stunning dome and a portrait of Chairman Mao on its façade has been converted into a Spanish restaurant, the Ashanti Dome.

Just south of Fuxing Park along Sinan Lu (the former rue Masenet) are two of Shanghai's many historic residences, the former homes of major Revolutionary political figures, now serving as museums. The **Former Residence of Sun Yat-sen** (7 Xiangshan Lu at Sinan Lu; <www.sh-sunyat-sen.com>; open daily 9am–4.30pm; admission fee) contains memorabilia of the founder of the Chinese Republic, who lived in this small mansion with his wife, Soong Qing-ling, from 1918 to 1924. Just down the block is the **Former Residence of Zhou Enlai** (73 Sinan Lu; open daily 9–11am, 1–5pm; admission fee). Chairman Mao's second-in-charge occupied this more modest house in 1946. Premier Zhou's black Buick is kept here.

At the southern end of Sinan Lu is **Taikang Lu Art Street**, a project begun in 1988 to convert factories and other buildings along Taikang Lu into studios, galleries and lofts for local artists, fashion designers and craftworkers. The best-known gallery here is the **Deke Erh Centre** (Building 2B, Lane 210, Taikang Lu; <www.han-yuan.com>; open daily 9.30am–5.30pm), a warehouse manned by local photographer, painter and publisher Deke Erh, best known for his books on Shanghai's architecture. Nearby is another Deke Erh institution, the Old China Hand Reading Room (27 Shaoxing Lu at Shaanxi Nan Lu; open daily 10am–midnight), where reading can be combined with a cup of coffee or tea.

Another short walk south, but far from any Metro station, is the **Museum of Public Security** (518 Ruijin Nan Lu; open Mon–Sat 8.30am–4pm; admission fee), a collection related to the history of crime and detection in Shanghai, with grisly photographs, confiscated pistols, skulls, opium pipes and gangster paraphernalia.

Museum of Public Security

Maoming Nan Lu

Just as Huaihai Nan Lu served as the French Concession's main east–west boulevard, Maoming Nan Lu (the former rue Cardinal Mercier) and the parallel Ruijin Er Lu (the former Route Père Robert) were the most crowded north–south streets. The Maoming/Ruijin area is still the busiest in the French Concession, teeming with bars, cafés, shops, hotels, mansions, villas and historic sites.

The **Ruijin Guesthouse**, two blocks south of Huaihai Zhong Lu at 118 Ruijin Er Lu, occupies the walled estate of H. E. Morris Jr, son of the founder of pre-Revolutionary China's largest daily English-language newspaper. The lush estate once housed horse stables and greyhound kennels. The surviving 1930s red-brick villas and mansions now serve as a hotel and various restaurants, including the stylish Faces bar in the exquisite colonial mansion known prosaically as Build-

Jingwen Flower Market

ing No. 4. Just west of this quintessential colonial estate are the remains of the canidrome where Morris raced his dogs, now occupied in part by the **Jingwen Flower Market** (225 Shaanxi Nan Lu; open daily 8am–8pm).

The south end of Maoming Nan Lu is notorious for its late-night bar and disco scene, while the north end is packed with historical

The Lyceum Theatre

sights. The **Cathay Theatre** (870 Huaihai Zhong Lu) sets the tone with its 1930s Art Deco spire and interiors. It still screens Chinese-language movies. Another block north is another historic stage still in operation, the **Lyceum Theatre** (57 Maoming Nan Lu), where the ballerina Margot Fonteyn, daughter of a colonial expat, danced as a girl before returning to England aged 14. The Lyceum was opened in 1931 by the British Consul for the Amateur Dramatics Society, but today it is more likely to host a visiting rock group than a Shakespearean ensemble.

Between the Cathay and Lyceum theatres are two pages out of French Concession history. The **Okura Garden Hotel** (58 Maoming Nan Lu) is a modern structure that delicately swallowed the Cercle Sportif Française, a luxurious 1926 private club. Preserved in the hotel's east wing are the original marble staircase, bawdily carved colonnades and the Grand Ballroom, its ceiling panelled in stained glass. The hotel garden was also originally part of the club and its tennis courts conceal a concrete nuclear bunker installed during the Cold War at the behest of Chairman Mao, who used the club as a private residence when he was in Shanghai.

Directly across the street is a large survivor from colonial days, the legendary **Jin Jiang Hotel** (59 Maoming Nan Lu). Opened as Cathay Mansions in 1928 by Victor Sassoon (of Peace Hotel fame), it became part of a larger hotel complex in 1951. In 1972 US President Nixon and Chinese Premier Zhou Enlai signed the Shanghai Communiqué here, opening Communist China's doors to the West. The shopping lane just inside the Jin Jiang's wall, no longer as stylish as it was a decade ago, still has some interesting stores and restaurants.

JINGAN

North of the French Concession and west of Renmin Square, Jingan District became an official part of the International Settlement in 1899, connected to the racetrack (now Renmin Park) by Bubbling Well Road. The main street in modern times is the same, but it is now called Nanjing Xi Lu, the western extension of Nanjing Road. Here are several of the city's most upmarket shopping malls (CITIC Square, Westgate Mall, Plaza 66) and its leading hotel-residence complex, Shanghai Centre (at 1376 Nanjing Xi Lu), which contains not only the 40-storey Portman Ritz-Carlton Hotel, but a luxury theatre, a shopping centre with its own Starbucks and an international supermarket, designer-name boutiques (Cartier, Cirutti, Louis Vuitton), airline offices, a bank and a medical clinic.

Jade Buddha in Yufo Si

The district also contains some colonial mansions and villas of note, as well as two of Shanghai's most important Buddhist temples. The one temple most often shown to tour groups in Shanghai is **Yufo Si**, the **Jade Buddha Temple** (170 Anyuan Lu; open daily 8am–4.30pm; admission fee), although it is certainly not one of China's more spectacular temple complexes. An active Zen Buddhist shrine today, the temple dates back only to 1882, with the present halls constructed from 1918 to 1920. The focal points are two white jade Buddha statues carved from a single slab of Burmese jade, one sitting, one reclining.

Jingan District's other temple of note has a much longer history. **Jingan Temple** (1686 Nanjing Xi Lu; open daily 7.30am–5pm; admission fee) dates from the 4th century AD and presides over an enormous Ming Dynasty copper bell, the 'bubbling well' for which the district is known and several stone Buddhas nearly as old as the temple. During the colonial period its abbot epitomised the times, keeping seven mistresses and ruling over worshippers like a godfather. Jingan Temple

Jingan Temple celebration

> **Shanghai residents' claim to be a part of the international middle class is substantiated by the numerous Starbucks cafés (more than in most US cities) and the presence of an IKEA home-furnishings store, complete with smorgasbord (126 Caoxi Lu).**

has monks and active worshippers, but is undergoing thorough reconstruction, and seems destined to become a temple marketplace rather than a historic shrine.

Across the street is charming **Jingan Park** (open dawn to after midnight; free). Rebuilt in 1999, it encompasses a Metro station, courtyard shopping, a classical garden pond, morning *tai chi* classes and a Sunday morning 'English corner' where Chinese students linger, hoping to practise their language skills with foreigners.

Children's Municipal Palace

Soong Qing-ling, China's honorary president and city resident, created the concept of children's palaces, after-school programmes for gifted children seeking advanced instruction in disciplines ranging from calligraphy to photography. Of several dozen such extracurricular schools in Shanghai, the most popular is the **Children's Municipal Palace** (64 Yan An Xi Lu; tel: 021 6248 1850; open Mon–Fri 4.30–6pm, Sat–Sun 9am–4pm; free). Visitors usually require an appointment or need to join a local tour group. The students, aged 6–16, often entertain foreigners in their classrooms as they sing, dance or hone their computer skills. The building would be worth seeing even if the students weren't on hand to delight. Known in old Shanghai as the Marble Hall, it was built from 1918 to 1931 as a private mansion by Sir Elly Kadoorie, a Baghdad Jew who became Shanghai's leading taipan. This was the first air-conditioned house in Shanghai, resplendent with Italian marble fireplace mantels, immense chandeliers and a grand ballroom with 19-m (65-ft) vaulted ceilings.

Ohel Rachel Synagogue

A second monument to the Jewish community in colonial Shanghai is the **Ohel Rachel Synagogue** (500 Shaanxi Bei Lu; closed), just inside the main gate of the Shanghai Education Commission and visible from the street. Jacob Sassoon built the synagogue in memory of his wife Rachel in 1920; it was used until 1949 primarily by Shanghai's wealthy Sephardic Jewish residents. After 1949 the synagogue became a stable and a warehouse. In 1998 it was readied for a special visit from US First Lady Hillary Clinton and Secretary of State Madeleine Albright (who had lived as a girl in pre-Revolutionary Shanghai), but it has been closed since and now appears on the United Nations' list of the world's 100 most endangered monuments.

Shanghai Exhibition Centre

Exhibition Centre

In the early 1950s, the Soviet Union was Communist China's most helpful ally. The most visible sign of this alliance in Shanghai is the 1955 **Shanghai Exhibition Centre** (1000 Yan An Zhong Lu). Now a decaying, but still striking, Russian-built European palace, it hosts international exhibitions. The site once contained Hardoon Gardens, the private estate of Silas Hardoon, another Jewish millionaire from Baghdad, who owned more than 1,000 buildings in Shanghai when he died in 1931. Hardoon Gardens, designed by a local Buddhist monk, was completed in 1909, covered 12 hectares (30 acres) and contained a Buddhist college. Its western border, the former Hardoon Road, is today's Tongren Lu, recently reconstructed as a modern food street with trendy bars and cafés.

Former Residence of Chairman Mao

Chairman Mao Zedong occupied several different houses during the 1920s when he lived in Shanghai with his first wife and their two children, but the main abode is a now museum devoted to his early years, the **Former Residence of Chairman Mao** (120 Maoming Bei Lu; open Tues–Sun 9–11.30am, 1–4.30pm; admission fee includes English-speaking guide).

Former Residence of Chairman Mao

The two-storey brick *shikumen* (stone-gate) residence is immaculate and spare, with rooms on the first floor lightly furnished and the upstairs rooms displaying photos, letters and other documents that provide a chronology of Chairman Mao's life in the 1920s and the 1950s and 1960s. There's not a hint, however, of Mao's later wife, the notorious Madame Mao, who headed the Gang of Four during the Cultural Revolution (1966–76). The courtyard is often used to display marvellous propaganda posters celebrating the triumphs of the masses during the reign of the Great Helmsman.

XUHUI (SOUTHWEST SHANGHAI)

The French Concession overflows its formal western border of Shaanxi Nan Lu and spreads into the Xuhui District of southwest Shanghai. In fact, the northern section of this district has some of Shanghai's most remarkable colonial architecture, including many a lovely mansion. It is in this grand suburb of the French Concession that many of Shanghai's foreign consulates are located today.

Northern Xuhui's main boulevard is **Hengshan Lu**, a continuation of the French Concession's Huaihai Zhong Lu. Formerly the avenue Petain, Hengshan Lu has regained much of its colonial atmosphere thanks to an ambitious restoration programme that re-tiled the pavements, added wrought-ron railings and lampposts at intersections, and attracted trend-setting shops, restaurants and bars to restored villas and houses. The **International Community Church** (53 Hengshan Lu; tel: 021 6437 6576; Sunday services), also known as the Hengshan Community Church, fits right in with its ivy-covered walls. Opened in 1925, this is Shanghai's most active Protestant church.

Hengshan Lu is festooned with colonial mansions, some still used as multi-family residences or organisational headquarters, but a growing number are open to visitors as restaurants and shops. The English villa at 9 Dongping Lu, just off Hengshan Lu, was once the 'palace away from the palace' when China's Republican President, Chiang Kai-shek, visited with his renowned wife, Soong Mei-ling. Now called Sasha's, its doors are open to diners seeking Western meals and drinks. In yet another old French villa down a narrow side street, Le Garçon Chinois (Lane 9, Hengshan Lu at Dongping Lu) is a romantic little French café now serving Spanish fare.

Fenyang Lu

Among the more attractive streets branching off Hengshan Lu is **Fenyang Lu** (the former route Pichon), and among its more attractive mansions is the present-day Japanese restaurant, Ambrosia (150 Fenyang Lu), which occupies the three-storey villa built by a French merchant in 1930. The

Hengshan Lu

showpiece, however, is the **Shanghai Museum of Arts and Crafts** (79 Fenyang Lu; open daily 9am–4pm; admission fee), the quintessential, shimmering white colonial Shanghai mansion with its sweeping marble staircases, wood panelling, tiled fireplaces, stained glass and wide lawn and garden, all dating from 1905. Once the home of Shanghai's first Communist mayor, Chen Yi, it has provided studios for many fine artisans since

The 1925 mansion at Huaihai Zhong Lu and Donghu Lu was built by a Jewish merchant, owned by a Chinese crime lord and used at various times by actresses, police chiefs, Mao's wife and US President Nixon. A superbly preserved mansion, it opened to the public for the first time in 2002 as a Shanghaianese cuisine bar and restaurant, The 7.

1960. After recent minor restorations, the mansion is a museum of traditional crafts (bamboo, jade, ivory, embroidery, costumes, snuff bottles, paper lanterns), a gallery of master craftsmen at work and a retail outlet.

Fenyang is also a street of the arts, particularly of music. On the campus of the Shanghai Music Conservatory, the **Oriental Musical Instruments Museum** (20 Fenyang Lu; open Mon–Fri 9–11am, 1.30–5pm; admission fee) displays musical instruments of modern and ancient China and folk instruments of the world. Back on the street, keep an eye out for piano movers; Fenyang Lu is lined with Western musical instrument stores.

Xiangyang

Fenyang Lu merges with Huaihai Zhong Lu just west of Shanghai's biggest discount designer-label flea market, the impossibly crowded, irresistibly low-priced **Xiangyang Clothing Market** *(see page 84)*. Colonial Shanghai's most

Hengshan Moller Villa

bizarre mansion, **Hengshan Moller Villa**, now a hotel *(see page 132)*, lies a few blocks north from here, in the northeast corner of Xuhui District (at Shaanxi Nan Lu and Yan An Zhong Lu). Nearer the market is the **Cathedral of the Holy Mother of God** (55 Xinle Lu), a Russian Orthodox church that began serving White Russian refugees in 1931. It has more recently accommodated a branch of the stock exchange and an inexpensive restaurant, the Grape.

At 1555 Huaihai Zhong Lu, the **New Shanghai Library** (Shanghai Tushuguan; open daily 8am–8pm) is one of the world's largest libraries, with over 13 million volumes, rare books dating back 1,400 years and a reading room with foreign-language books.

At Xuhui's western edge is the **Former Residence of Soong Qing-ling** (1843 Huaihai Zhong Lu; open daily 9am–4.30pm; admission fee). This is the house where Soong Qing-ling lived following the death of her husband, the founder of modern China, Sun Yat-sen. Of the many former residences of historical personalities in Shanghai, this is the most interesting one. Soong Qing-ling was the only one of Shanghai's famous Soong sisters to stay in China after the Revolution in 1949 (her sister Soong Mei-ling fled to Taiwan with husband Chiang Kai-shek). She lived in this 1920s villa, built by a Greek sea captain, until 1963, when she moved to Beijing. Only the first floor is open to visitors; an annexe displays her diploma from Wesleyan College in the US, gramophone records and personal letters. The garage houses two classic Communist limousines from the 1950s, one Chinese, the other Russian (a gift from Stalin).

St Ignatius Cathedral

Just south of the Xujiahui Metro stop are all that remains of Shanghai's oldest Catholic community, known in the 1800s as Zi-ka-wei. **St Ignatius Cathedral** (158 Puxi Lu at Caoxi Bei Lu; open Sat–Sun 7.30–11am, 1–4pm), also known as Xujiahui Cathedral, is Shanghai's largest church, holding 3,000 worshippers. Opened in 1910, its 26-m (85-ft) high vaulted ceiling is supported by 64 stone Corinthian columns. The cathedral was closed in 1958 by the local Communist government and converted into an umbrella handle and pillowcase factory that employed several hundred nuns and priests until the late 1970s.

Xu Guang Qi (1562–1633), known as China's first astronomer, converted to Christianity after meeting Jesuit missionary Matteo Ricci. He established the first Western settlement in Shanghai, with churches on this site as early as 1608. Xu's tomb, slated for renovation, is just south of the present cathedral, in a park bearing his name.

Other surviving pieces of the Catholic complex in Xuhui include the recently reopened **Shanghai Library Bibliotheca Zi-ka-wei** (80 Caoxi Bei Lu; tel: 021 6487 4072 ext 107; open Mon–Sat 9am–4pm; free), located just north of the cathedral. The taller of the two library buildings was built in 1868 as a residence for Jesuit priests; the shorter, constructed in 1897, still houses a collection of over 100,000 Western books dating from the early 16th century.

South of the cathedral is the **Zi-ka-wei Observatory** (166 Puxi Lu), operated by French Jesuits from 1873 to 1949. Weather reports were once transmitted from here to the Signal Tower on the Bund *(see page 30)*. The four-storey red-brick observatory tower is closed to the public. The **Convent of the Holy Mother** (201 Caoxi Bei Lu), built in 1931, is open, however, although not as nunnery but as the Old Station Restaurant *(see page 141)*.

A young woman pins up her wish at Longhua Temple

Longhua Temple

Shanghai's largest and most vibrant Buddhist complex is **Longhua Temple** (2853 Longhua Lu; open daily 7am–5pm; admission fee), which is not often visited by foreigners, perhaps because it is so far from a Metro station. Longhua boasts Shanghai's tallest (44m/145ft) and most striking pagoda (Bao Ta), built during the Song

The Botanical Garden

Dynasty (AD 960–1279), much admired, but not open since the 1930s. The temple grounds contain many centuries-old halls, golden Buddhist statues and copious incense burners for the throngs of daily worshippers. The big bronze bell in the bell tower near the entrance gate can be struck three times for a fee.

Also seldom visited at the southern end of Xuhui District is a major horticultural display, the **Shanghai Botanical Garden** (1111 Longhua Lu; open daily 6am–5pm summer, 7.30am–4.30pm winter; admission fee). The large park (81 hectares/200 acres) is sectioned into gardens featuring many star attractions, from bamboo and osmanthus to peonies and much-prized orchids. The Bonsai Garden has thousands of well-displayed specimens.

CHANGNING

The Changning District extends west of the old International Settlement and French Concession to the Hongqiao Airport, which handles most of China's domestic flights. Its major east–west roads are Changning Lu, Hongqiao Lu and the Yan An Xi Lu elevated expressway. The district was opened to pioneering foreign investments in the 1980s, becoming known as the **Hongqiao Development Zone**. In the 1990s an entire modern residential town, Gubei, was built for the thousands of expatriate businessmen and their families, mainly Asians, who poured into Shanghai. Gubei now has its own ranks of good restaurants, shops and supermarkets, although there are no historic attractions and the Metro system has not yet been extended this far west.

Shanghai's best antique furniture warehouses are located near the airport on Hongqiao Lu and Wu Zhong Lu, as is tycoon Victor Sassoon's original country estate with its ponds, streams, pavilions and 1930s Tudor-style villa, now the Cypress Hotel (2419 Hongqiao Lu; tel: 021 6268 8868), but the district's major sightseeing draws are the zoo and a mausoleum.

For fans of Shanghai's historic celebrities, particularly of the Soong sisters, the **Soong Qing-ling Mausoleum** (21 Song Yuan Lu, south off Hongqiao Lu; open daily 8.30am–5pm; admission fee) is irresistible. An exhibition room of Soong's life and her tomb, next to those of her parents and her beloved maid, Li Yane, occupy the central portion of the

---

Animals in a Golf Club

Shanghai Zoo (2381 Hongqiao Lu; tel: 021 6268 7775; open daily Apr–Sep 6.30am–7pm, Oct–Mar 7am–5pm; admission fee; free for children under 1.2m/4ft) is one of the better zoological preserves in China, although by no means a state-of-the-art showpiece. It has 6,000 animals, of 600 species. The pandas have their own centre and are the chief draw, but there are also rare Chinese birds, crocodiles and the South China tiger, also known as the Amoy tiger. The 4.6-hectare (11-acre) grounds, formerly a British golf club, have places for picnicking, playgrounds and a Ferris wheel.

encompassing Wanguo International Cemetery. A larger-than-life white marble statue beside her grave is a frequent gathering point for schoolchildren on field trips, who bow at her image.

The International Cemetery has a western section devoted to Chinese political bigwigs and an eastern sector with about 700 plain markers for foreigners, the markers not original since the graveyard was demolished at the time of the

Soong Qing-ling Mausoleum

Cultural Revolution. Three members of millionaire Victor Sassoon's family have headstones here. The most exceptional monument, dedicated to Sir Elly Kadoorie (d. 1944) and his wife Lady Laura (d. 1918), bears the inscription, 'The true grave of the dead is in the heart of the living.'

HONGKOU (NORTH SHANGHAI)

The district north of the Bund, across Suzhou Creek, has a history of foreign residency, from American and Japanese colonialists to Russian and Jewish immigrants. The Suzhou Creek shoreline is still dominated by the Russian Consulate, its tenants unchanged since 1917; Shanghai Mansions, the former Broadway Mansions, opened in 1933; and the Pujiang Hotel, once the upmarket Astor House, built in 1911. The old warehouses and apartment blocks immediately east and north of the 'North Bund' are slated to disappear soon, however, as Shanghai goes into top gear to redevelop its shoreline for the 2010 World Expo.

Hongkou's other neighbourhood of interest to foreign visitors is in the vicinity of **Lu Xun Park**. Lu Xun (1881–1936) is considered the creator of modern Chinese literature and a revolutionary visionary. The **Former Residence of Lu Xun** (No. 9, Lane 132, Shanying Lu; open daily 9am–5pm; admission fee) is a 1924 mansion where the Chinese League of Left-wing Writers was formed in 1930. The **Lu Xun Memorial Hall** (146 Jiangwan Dong Lu, Lu Xun Park; open daily 9am–5pm; admission fee), created in 1999, displays Lu Xun's books, hats and even his death mask.

Nearby, a lane of 1920s residential *shikumen* architecture, **Duolun Lu** (at Shaanxi Bei Lu), has been restored as a 'cultural street' to commemorate the progressive writers and

---

Shanghai's Jewish Heritage

The urban renewal planned for the World Expo in 2010 might raze the blocks that became a Jewish ghetto when Shanghai welcomed up to 20,000 refugees fleeing the Nazis in the 1930s. Shanghai had previously seen a small community of wealthy Jews from the Middle East and then of Russian Jews fleeing first the Tsar and then the Red Army. In 1942, occupying Japanese forces confined Shanghai's Jews to a ghetto in Hongkou. The main street was Huashan Lu, its townhouses now home to Chinese families. The most important surviving structure is the Ohel Moshe Synagogue, built in 1927 by Russian Jews and now housing the **Jewish Refugee Museum** (3rd floor, Ohel Moshe Synagogue, 62 Changyang Lu; open daily 9am–4.30pm; admission fee). It has only a few books and photos, but Wang Faliang, the overseer, can speak for hours about his memories of the Jewish residents who came here to worship more than half a century ago. There are a few hundred Jews here today, who can be contacted at the Shanghai Jewish Center (1720 Hongqiao Lu, No. 1 Shang-Mira Garden Villa; tel: 021 6278 0225; <www.chinajewish.org>).

Deliveries along the Duolun Lu

artists who once lived there. This curving cobblestone lane was opened as a pedestrian mall in 1998. The Duolun Art Gallery (at No. 27) has made a splash with its provocative shows; the Great Virtue Christian Church (No. 59), built in 1928, has been converted to art shops; a French mansion now serves as a coin museum; the Old Film Café (No. 123) shows vintage movies; and numerous curio shops hawk chopsticks, porcelain and (at No. 183) Mao badges from a stock of 10,000.

PUDONG (EAST SHANGHAI)

The development of Pudong is key to Shanghai's bid to become the economic capital of Asia and one of the world's great cities. In 1900 Pudong was little more than mudflats, warehouses, petrol tank farms and rural townships, with no access except by water. Today Pudong shines across the Huangpu River as the Shanghai of skyscrapers, boldly new,

Oriental Pearl TV Tower

boldly Western, boldly commercial. By no means is all of Pudong as developed as its shoreline area, officially known as the Lujiazui Financial and Trade Zone. Pudong stretches all the way out to the Pudong International Airport and the East China Sea, covering 500 sq km (200 sq miles), much of it still rural; but the predominant note east of the river is financial, commercial and industrial. Pudong is east Shanghai, the city of China's future.

Oriental Pearl TV Tower and Around

Pudong already has some worthy attractions for visitors who have come to see rather than invest in China's future. An overall perspective of Shanghai, east and west, is afforded by Pudong's modern landmark, the **Oriental Pearl TV Tower** (1 Shi Ji Da Dao; open daily 9am–9pm; admission fee). This iconic observation post, completed in 1994, is Asia's highest radio and TV tower, at 468m (1,535ft). Looking like a gargantuan children's toy, with its tubes, bubbles and spire, it offers a rotating buffet restaurant halfway up and a dazzling panorama in the top bubble (at 350m/1,100ft), subject to haze and clouds.

The basement of the tower contains the **Shanghai Municipal History Museum** (Gate 4, Oriental Pearl TV Tower, 1 Shi Ji Da Dao; open daily 9am–9pm; admission fee). The focus here is on colonial Shanghai (1842–1949), with artefacts, dioramas and photographs that evoke the romantic city of the past, including its trolley cars, wedding palanquins, brothels, shop houses and opium dens.

From the tower it is an easy walk northeast to the **Shanghai Ocean Aquarium** *(see page 94)*, Asia's largest, and northwest to the hands-on **Natural Wild Insect Kingdom** *(see page 94)*. Directly west is Pudong's version of the Bund, the 2.5km (1½-mile) **Riverside Promenade** (east shore, Huangpu River; open daily dawn to midnight; free). The views of the river and the Bund are spectacular, particularly after dark, and Starbucks, Häagen-Dazs and others have staked out alfresco locations along the riverfront.

East of the TV tower is the **Lujiazui Central Green**, 100,000 sq m (1 million sq ft) of lawn for kite-flying and picnicking, and just beyond, a colonial remnant, the **Lujiazui Development Museum** (15 Lujiazui Lu; open daily 10am–5pm; admission fee). This 1917 courtyard mansion,

Reptiles at the Natural Wild Insect Kingdom

the home of a wealthy Chinese merchant, is a wonderfully restored anomaly, with a few displays and artefacts related to the development of the district.

Across the wide main boulevard, Shi Ji Da Dao, is China's tallest building and most graceful skyscraper, the **Jinmao Tower** (2 Shi Ji Da Dao; open daily 9am–9pm; admission fee). Rising 88 storeys to a height of 421m (1,379ft), it has the segmented appearance of a modern pagoda or bamboo shoot. The Grand Hyatt Hotel occupies floors 51 to 88, making it the world's highest hotel. The observation deck on top has views to rival those of the Oriental Pearl TV Tower. Eventually the view will be obscured, or perhaps made more interesting, with the completion of the building next door, the Shanghai World Financial Centre, planned to top out at 472m (1,548ft), making it the world's tallest skyscraper, with 101 storeys.

On Zhang Yang Lu in Pudong is the Yaohan Department Store, known as **Ba Bai Ban**. It is probably the largest shop in all Asia, standing 10 storeys high and selling everything from clothing to cars.

Pudong's **Century Boulevard** (Shi Ji Da Dao) ties Pudong's towers together and gives this new Shanghai the

Museum Boom

By the year 2010, when Shanghai hosts the World Expo, the city aims to have 100 museums. The ambitious plans focus on Pudong, which expects to open a museum of traditional Chinese medicine, an electricity museum (Shanghai's first 15 arc lamps appeared on the Bund as early as 1882), a banking museum (in the ICBC Building, 9 Pudong Da Dao) and a massive railway museum complete with steam locomotives, to be located on the site of the old North Train Station at 80 Tianmu Dong Lu.

feel of a Los Angeles of the East. Running eight lanes wide for 4km (2½ miles), it sweeps southwards to the sparkling new **Science and Technology Museum** *(see page 94)* and mammoth **Century Park** *(see page 94)*.

At the Longyang Lu Metro station is the western terminus of the Maglev (open Mon–Fri 8.30am–12.30pm, Sat–Sun 8.30am–5.30pm), which transports those in a hurry to meet flights at the Pudong Airport by reaching the space-age cruising speed of 430km/h (265 mph). This German-engineered magnetic levitation train is the fastest, most expensive public transit device in the world, an apt symbol of Shanghai's high-speed dreams of its place in the new millennium.

THE WATER TOWNS

While old Shanghai is almost completely confined to what survives from the colonial period (the 1840s onwards), until recently the outlying counties have been largely untouched by Westernisation and modern development. The gardens, temples, canals, bridges and mansions outside the city frequently predate anything inside the urban boundaries. The vast Yangzi River delta was criss-crossed for centuries by canals feeding the Grand Canal, and a number of old towns along the canals now provide idyllic retreats for a day-trip into

Plying the canals

the region's pre-colonial past. Travellers can book escorted group tours of these 'water towns' from hotel desks and travel agencies, or they can rough it by booking a seat on one of the early-morning Shanghai City sightseeing buses (Staircase 5, Gate 12, Shanghai Stadium, 666 Tianyaoqiao Lu, Xuhui District; tel: 021 6426 5555), some of which have Chinese-speaking guides and lunches included in their inexpensive fares.

Zhouzhuang

This 900-year-old water village 80km (50 miles) south-west of Shanghai is the most popular of the canal towns

Visitors crowd the ancient waterways of Zhouzhuang

(over 2 million visitors annually), hence the most crowded with visitors. Its waterways, arched bridges, gondolas and historic residences are quite picturesque, however, resembling a scene on an antique blue willow dinner plate. The town canals once linked Shanghai to the Grand Canal for the shipment of rice, silk and ceramics to the northern capital of Beijing. The canals are now jammed with gondolas filled with tourists and propelled by local peasant women at the tillers. The houses, the majority of which date from Ming- and Qing-dynasty days, are rambling residences. The **Shen Residence**, built in 1742, consists of more than 100 rooms, while the 70-room **Zhang Residence** is even older, dating from 1449. Both are open to visitors.

While Zhouzhuang seems centuries removed from Shanghai, in fact the big city's modern entrepreneurial spirit has swept across the delta. Developers in this water town have begun construction of **Shangduli** , an entertainment complex comparable to Shanghai's Xintiandi, with restaurants, boutiques, theatres, nightclubs and a golf course. Promoters have promised to preserve the ancient flavour of 'Shanghai's Venice', but at the same time make Zhouzhuang 'more vibrant'.

Tongli

This Song Dynasty water town near Suzhou, 80km (49 miles) west of Shanghai, is an increasingly popular delta destination. It consists of seven islands connected by 15 waterways and some 49 arched bridges. Gondolas for hire ply the waterways, while Ming- and Qing-dynasty wooden houses, the largest consisting of over 40 rooms, flank the lanes. The main attraction is Tuisi Garden, a 19th-century classical Chinese garden that is now on the UNESCO World Heritage list.

Nanxun

One of the least-visited water towns, Nanxun, 123km (74 miles) west of Shanghai, is perched on the shores of Lake Tai. The town dates from the 13th century. Its waterways are traversed by gondolas for hire. The **Little Lotus Villa**, built in 1885 by a rich merchant who made a fortune in the silk trade, is a fine classical garden and private estate. The influence of French colonialists is embodied in the **Zhang Residence**, built in 1905, which features a European ballroom. The town's One Hundred Rooms River is lined with Ming-Dynasty terrace houses, still homes to local residents who have added power lines and satellite TV dishes.

Ancient Sex on Display

China's first and only sex museum, squeezed out of central Shanghai, has ended up in an unlikely spot, the water village of Tongli, and in unlikely quarters as well – the Li Ze Girls' School. The **Chinese Ancient Sex Culture Museum** (Wu Jiang, Tongli; tel: 0512 6332 2972; open daily 7.45am–5.30pm; admission fee) is the result of Professor Liu Dalin's passion to document 5,000 years of sexuality in China, illustrated in the museum by over 4,000 artefacts, ranging from foot-binding apparatus to erotic scrolls and sexual aids in stone and porcelain.

EXCURSIONS FROM SHANGHAI

She Shan

Shanghai's most magnificent cathedral stands atop a 100-m (300-ft) hill 30km (18 miles) southwest of the city in the She Shan National Forest Park. **She Shan Cathedral** (open daily dawn to dusk) was built by French Jesuit missionaries in 1871 and later rebuilt in its present form (1925–35). Once known as the Basilica Minor of St Mary, it became the destination of an annual May pilgrimage devoted to the Virgin. Pilgrims journeyed up the south side of the forested peak, passing shrines marking the stations of the cross. The stations along this Via Dolorosa remain. A statue of the Madonna and Child crowns the 38-m (125-ft) bell tower, a replacement for the original pulled down by the Red Guards during the Cultural Revolution. In 1983 local Chinese Catholics were instrumental in reopening the cathedral, which is still devoted to the Virgin Mary. A seminary now houses over 100 priests in training.

She Shan Cathedral

The building is open to visitors and worshippers alike. The cathedral's interior is plain and clean, its arched ceiling supported by white granite pillars. As well as the Via Dolorosa, a

Zo-Se Jesuit Observatory

cable car and wide stairway also lead to the cathedral from the north side.

Adjoining the cathedral is a modern observatory (closed to the public) and, in neat counterpoint, the old **Zo-Se Jesuit Observatory** (open daily 9am–4pm; free), founded in 1900 by the French Catholic Mission from the Xujiahui Cathedral and Zi-Ka-Wei Observatory in Shanghai. Under the big metal dome is an enormous telescope, manufactured in Paris in 1898, complete with an attached chair on a circular track for the astronomer. The telescope (a 40-cm/16-inch refractor with a double 6.9-m/22½-ft tube) is still in use. The observatory is an astronomical museum with old instruments and photographs on display, including images from large glass plates of Halley's Comet (1910 and 1986) taken through the old telescope.

On the nearby peak of Tianmashan, some 8km (5 miles) from She Shan, is the 'Leaning Tower of China', the **Huzhu Pagoda** (open daily dawn to dusk; free). Erected in 1079, the seven-storey, 20-m (60-ft) eight-sided dark brick tower out-leans the more famous Leaning Tower of Pisa. Reinforced in 1985, it has a forlorn and haunting look. A long trail leads through bamboo forests to a Buddhist temple and the Huzhu Pagoda near the summit, which is about the same height as She Shan. Three halls beside the leaning pagoda contain Buddhist statues, but it is not an active temple.

Independent travellers can reach She Shan on Bus No. 1B from the City Sightseeing Bus Centre in Shanghai (Staircase 5, Gate 12, Shanghai Stadium, 666 Tianyaoqiao Lu, Xuhui District; tel: 021 6426 5555). Hotel desks and local travel agents offer day tours of She Shan with English-speaking guides.

Suzhou

Marco Polo dubbed **Suzhou** the 'Venice of the East' when he passed through in the late 13th century, and the city, 80km (50 miles) northwest of Shanghai, retains the network of canals and the legion of private classical Chinese gardens that have made Suzhou a byword for beauty. Suzhou is near enough to Shanghai to create a spate of day-trip and overnight options that can be booked at hotel desks or through travel agencies. It is also served by nearly hourly

Canalside houses in Suzhou

The delights of a Suzhou garden

departures from the Shanghai Railway Station and a week-end service from the City Sightseeing Bus Centre (Staircase 5, Gate 12, Shanghai Stadium, 666 Tianyaoqiao Lu, Xuhui District; tel: 021 6426 5555). The chief attractions are the gardens, the canals and the silk business that made Suzhou a much richer, more cultured city than Shanghai in pre-colonial days. Suzhou's inner city retains its historical appearance (no skyscrapers allowed), crisscrossed by more than 30km (20 miles) of canals, with a dozen of China's best gardens open to the public.

In Suzhou, the China International Travel Service (18 Dajing Xiang Lu; tel: 0512 6522 3783) can arrange city guides and tours. The leading hotel is the Sheraton Suzhou Hotel & Tower (259 Xin Shi Lu, Pan Men Gate; tel: 0512 6510 3388; <www.sheraton.com/suzhou>).

Suzhou's tiny jewel, **Master of the Nets Garden** (Wang-shi Yuan, 11 Kuotao Xiang off Shiquan Jie; open daily

8am–4.30pm; admission fee), is the considered a master-piece of Chinese garden design. Its maze of halls, walls and bamboo screens gives it an infinite variety of perspectives, despite the diminutive size of the garden. All the elements are here: stone bridges, goldfish pond, rockeries, courtyards and the owner's 18th-century pavilion, furnished simply with scrolls, lanterns and a writing desk. Throughout the summer, traditional music and dance are staged nightly.

Humble Administrator's Garden (Zhouzheng Yuan, 178 Dongbei Jie; open daily 7.30am–5pm; admission fee) is the city's largest horticultural estate. It was built by a wealthy Mandarin in 1509. Bridges link its lakes and isles, and perfectly placed pavilions provide shifting vistas across artfully arranged 'natural' spaces.

Goldfish in the Master of the Nets Garden

Stone slabs are a hallmark of Chinese classical gardens, especially in Suzhou's **Lingering Garden** (Liu Yuan, 80 Liu Yuan Lu; open daily 7.30am–5pm; admission fee). These natural monuments were dredged from nearby Tai Lake (Tai Hu), which pocked and contorted the stone slabs into the shapes of fantastical mountain peaks. The most celebrated of these Tai Hu

For the first time in modern history Suzhou officials decided in 2005 to auction off one of their famous classical gardens to the highest bidder. The minimum bid for Feng Mei Cottage, a 1,874 sq m (½ acre) property, was 56 million yuan (about $7 million/£4 million).

rocks, called Crown of Clouds Peak, is now located in Lingering Garden; it weighs in at 5 tonnes and measures 6m (20ft) from tip to base.

Tai Hu rocks, many of which resemble lions, are also a prominent feature of the **Grove of the Lions Garden** (Shizilin Yuan, 23 Yuan Lin Lu; open daily 7.30am–5pm; admission fee), the creation of a Buddhist monk in 1342. This spacious garden contains four lakes, numerous pavilions and the largest rock slabs and rockeries in Suzhou.

Drummers at Tiger Hill

Northwest of central Suzhou, **Tiger Hill** (8 Huqiu Shan; open daily 8am–6pm; admission fee) is part temple complex, part amusement park. Its centrepiece is the Cloud Rock Pagoda (Yunyan Ta), built in AD961 and now leaning a bit. It is believed to be the tomb of the King of Wu, founder of Suzhou.

On the southern edge of town, the **Pan Men Water Gate** (1 Dong Da Jie; open daily 8am–5pm; admission fee), built in 1351, once controlled the flow of barge traffic in and out of the Suzhou city wall, of which this tower is the last remaining piece. Nearby is a massive arched stone bridge, Wumen Qiao, under which canal traffic still navigates the waterway; and the Ruiguang Pagoda, dating from 1119, which was recently opened to the public and can be climbed for a fee.

Suzhou's famous city canals, which are periodically cleaned up for the tourist trade, can be viewed on foot or by small boat tours that leave from the wharves on Guang Ji Lu at the north end of town near the railway station.

The **Suzhou Silk Museum** (661 Renmin Lu; tel: 0512 6753 6538; open daily 9am–5pm; admission fee) displays the history of silk production, which first made Suzhou a power during the Tang Dynasty (AD618–907). The highlight is a working reproduction of a 13th-century silk farm, with worms, cocoons and mulberry leaves.

The **Suzhou History Museum** (204 Dongbei Jie; open daily 8.15am–4pm; admission fee), with artefacts dating back 6,000 years, replaces the old facility with an expansive pavilion of galleries designed by I. M. Pei.

Hangzhou

When the Song Dynasty moved its capital to Hangzhou in the 12th century, this city on the lake rapidly became one of China's leading centres of the silk trade and high culture. Its focus was West Lake (Xihu), the most beautiful lake in eastern China. Marco Polo pronounced Hangzhou a 'paradise', and West Lake remains a splendid attraction.

Central Hangzhou fans out from the eastern shore of the lake. There, **Hubin Lu Pedestrian Street**, a lakeside promenade anchored by a Starbucks, attracts strolling visitors, as does the adjacent **Xihutiandi** (West Lake Heaven and Earth), an upmarket pedestrian mall of restaurants and shops modelled closely on Shanghai's Xintiandi *(see page 42)*. East of the shoreline, the newly remodelled Qing Hefang Historical Street houses teashops, folk arts and crafts stores, restaurants and the Huqingyutang Chinese Medicine Museum (95 Dajingxiang Lu; open daily 8.45am–3.45pm; admission fee), its exhibits displayed in the 1870s courtyard mansion of a herbal chemist.

Day-trips or overnight packages to Hangzhou, 170km (105 miles) southwest of Shanghai, can be booked at hotel desks or through travel agencies. It is also served by frequent daily departures from the Shanghai Railway Station or from the City Sightseeing Bus Centre (Staircase 5, Gate 12, Shanghai Stadium, 666 Tianyaoqiao Lu, Xuhui District; tel: 021 6426 5555). The Zhejiang China International Travel Service (1 Shi Han Lu; tel: 0571 8505 9025) can arrange city guides and tours. There is also a hotline to help visitors (tel: 0571 96123). The leading hotel is the historic Shangri-La Hotel Hangzhou on the northwest shore (78 Bei Shan Lu; tel: 0571 8797 7951; <www.shangri-la.com>).

Hangzhou's famed **West Lake**, first dredged out during the Tang Dynasty, is 5km (3 miles) in diameter and crossed by two ancient causeways open to pedestrians only. The Bai Causeway (Baiti), named after a local 9th-century poet, runs

West Lake

parallel to the north shore. On its western end, connected to the shore by the Xiling Bridge, is Solitary Island, where Emperor Qian Long built a palace and viewing pavilions in 1773.

Solitary Island is now the location of the **Seal Engraver's Society** (free admission), which has displays of old stone carvings and chops; and the **Zhejiang Provincial Museum** (25 Gu Shan Lu; open Mon noon–4pm, Tues–Sun 9am–4pm; admission fee), with its ancient bronzes, ceramics and the skeleton of a whale stranded nearby in 1282, according to one account. The Bai Causeway continues for nearly 1km (½ mile) towards central Hangzhou, giving fine views of the lake and green hillsides.

> The Song-Dynasty poet Su Dongpo likened West Lake to one of ancient China's greatest beauties, Xizi – who was also calm, soft, delicate and enchanting. The girls of Hangzhou are still famous for their light, clear complexion, which is attributed to the mild, humid climate.

The Su Causeway, three times as long as the Bai Causeway, connects the north and south shores of West Lake, running parallel to the western shore. Beginning at the **Yue Fei Mausoleum** (Bei Shan Lu; open daily 7.30am–5.30pm; admission fee), a shrine commemorating a Song-Dynasty general, it permits close views of the fairytale islets, as well as entrance to the peony gardens and fish pools of **Flower Harbour Park** (open daily 8am–6pm; admission fee).

Boat tours of West Lake are highly popular. Water taxis can be hired, at negotiated prices, along the lake shore, and on Solitary Island and the Hubin Lu Pedestrian Walkway there are ticket booths for rowing boats, junks and small ferries. The common destination is the Island of Small Seas in the middle of the lake. Created in 1607, the island is shaped like a wheel, its four spokes demarcating four lotus

Peak that Flew from Afar

ponds. At the hub is a zigzag bridge leading to the **Flower and Bird Pavilion** (open daily 8am–5pm; admission fee), which has carved wooden screens, tea service and a view of the Three Pools Mirroring the Moon, three small water pagodas placed here in 1621, that seem to float on the lake surface.

Two pagodas overlook the lake from opposite sides. The Protecting Chu Pagoda (Baochu Ta) atop Precious Stone Hill on the lake's north shore was rebuilt in 1933. Its courtyard, filled with locals seeking outdoor exercise, provides a good overlook. On the southeast shore, a new tower, Thunder Peak Pagoda or Leifeng Ta (15 Nanshan Lu; open daily 8am–5.30pm, to 10pm in summer; admission fee), was opened in 2003. This up-to-date pagoda features an escalator, an archaeological museum and sweeping views of the lake, the tea hills and the blossoming skyscrapers of central Hangzhou.

Founded in AD326, the **Lingyin Temple** (Lingyin Si Lu; open daily dawn–dusk; admission fee), west of West Lake, is a Zen Buddhist shrine more grand than any in downtown Shanghai – and more spectacular. The limestone ridge of the mountain facing the temple, known as the Peak that Flew from Afar (Feilai Feng), is inscribed with over 300 holy images carved by monks and artists during the 13th and 14th centuries, while caves here contain images from as early as the 10th century.

The tea grown in the hills west of West Lake is among the most highly regarded in China. The first crop of Longjin tea, usually harvested in early April, is the most flavourful and most expensive (over 100 yuan/$12.50 per ounce). The **Dragon Well Tea Park** (Longjing Lu, southwest of West Lake; open daily 8am–5.30pm; admission fee) offers a chance to experience a traditional Chinese tea ceremony, buy local teas and meet local growers, some of whom invite visitors to their homes for more tea and tea sales. Closer in, the **China Tea Museum** (Longjing Lu; open daily 8.30am–4.45pm; free) outlines the history and customs of tea.

South of West Lake, the **China National Silk Museum** (73-1 Yu Huang Shan Lu; open daily 8am–6pm; free) exhibits clothing from many of China's dynasties, silkworms and looms, while at the same time selling clothing off the rack and fine Hangzhou silk from the bolt.

Dragon Well Tea Park

WHAT TO DO

Shanghai has a multitude of museums, but it is best known as China's leader in nightlife, fashions and shopping. For current entertainment listings, consult the free weekly and monthly English-language magazines available in hotels and cafés that are designed for expatriates and tourists, including *8 Days* (<www.8days.sh>), *That's Shanghai* (<www.thatssh.com>), *City Weekend* (<www.cityweekend.com.cn>) and *Shanghai Talk*. The free English-language newspaper *Shanghai Daily* also lists exhibitions and performances.

SHOPPING

Shanghai's shops, as well as its citizens, have long been regarded by the Chinese as the nation's most fashionable. The department stores offer the latest goods and these days the renovated shopping streets stock top-line boutique wear and trendy international items. For most travellers, however, Shanghai's prime shopping experience is to be found in the free-wheeling outdoor markets, filled with exotic Chinese wares and designer-label Western apparel.

Markets

Shanghai's many outdoor markets are packed with shoppers, but the goods require close inspection and dedicated bargaining. 'Antiques' are usually fakes, as are designer-label sportswear, shoes and a variety of commodities such as top-of-the-range watches and sets of golf clubs. Buyers must beware not only of claims of authenticity, but of inflated prices. Items that cannot be bargained down to a third of their original asking price are poor deals. Markets usually have numer-

A performance of *The Legend of the Red Lantern*

ous stalls offering the same item, so shop around. While browsing, keep your valuables secure, since Shanghai's pick-pockets frequent street markets and target foreigners.

The **Xiangyang Clothing Market** (Huaihai Zhong Lu at Xiangyang Lu; open daily 9am–9pm) in the Xuhui District contains the city's largest collection of designer-label apparel. The North Face gear, Nike shoes, Louis Vuitton handbags and the like, along with the Callaway golf clubs and Rolex watches, may be factory seconds, knock-offs (copies) or out-right fakes, but the prices are irresistible, and some of the merchandise in the hundreds of stalls might be the real thing.

The **Dongtai Lu Antiques Market** (Dongtai Lu at Liuhuekou Lu, Luwan District; open daily 9am–5pm) has Shanghai's largest display of collectibles. Locals say that there are no real antiques here (genuine pre-1949 merchandise must have a red-wax seal to clear Customs), but fakes or not, the merchandise stuffed into the hundreds of stalls and the shops behind them is intriguing. Mao buttons and Mao-era posters, porcelain, jewellery, baskets, furniture, wood carvings and curios all make solid Shanghai souvenirs.

The **Fuyou Market** (upper floors, 457 Fangbang Zhong Lu, Yuyuan Bazaar; open Sat–Sun 5am–6pm), also known as the

The Price of Friendship

Benchmark prices can be found at the **Shanghai Friendship Store** (68 Jinling Dong Lu, off the Bund; open daily 9.30am–9.30pm). This government-run emporium carries a full line of Chinese goods of reasonable quality, including antiques, arts and crafts, books, jewellery, clothing, cloisonné, carpets, silk, ceramics, scrolls, tea, furniture and Chinese souvenirs. These are items that are more expensive in upmarket department stores and boutiques, but cheaper in markets and local shops.

Ghost Market, starts at dawn when hundreds of traders spread out their attic treasures including coins, books, statues, snuff bottles, tea sets, jade pieces and painted scrolls. There are also plenty of newly churned-out factory fakes. A few blocks east (Basement, 265 Fangbang Zhong Lu) is a similar market, brimming with old collectibles, that spills out into the courtyard of the Temple of the Town God on weekends.

The **Dongjiadu Fabric Market** (Dongjiadu Lu and Zhongshan Nan Lu, Nanshi District; open daily 9am–5pm) is located far from any Metro station, but for bar-

Dongjiadu Fabric Market

gain hunters in search of bolts of Chinese silk, wool, cotton or cashmere, it is worth the taxi fare. Scores of stalls ensure a wide variety of patterns and extremely low prices, although synthetics and blends are sometimes passed off as silks or fine wools. Inexpensive tailors are on duty.

The merchandise at many street markets is not easy to pack or ship home. The warehouse of the **Jingwen Flower Market** (225 Shaanxi Nan Lu, French Concession; open daily 8am–8pm), for example, overflows with orchids, fresh flowers and house plants, as does the **Gubei Flower and Bird Market** (Gubei Nan Lu, Changning District; open daily 8am–6pm), but both locations are fascinating. So too is the **Dajing Lu Market** (Dajing Lu at Luxiangyuan Jie; open daily dawn to late after-

The No. 1 Department Store

noon), located four blocks west of the Yuyuan Bazaar near the last remnant of the old city wall. Dajing Lu is a vivid remnant of the city's old neighbourhoods, where vegetables, meat and seafood are snapped up by locals every morning.

Avenues and Malls

For decades the streets of central Shanghai have been a shopper's paradise of tiny shops, a tradition that persists despite a shift to malls and mega-stores. Shanghai's two main shopping thoroughfares are the legendary Nanjing Road, now largely favoured by tourists, and Huaihai Zhong Lu, a parallel avenue that locals favour. Both streets contain several kilometres of shopping, with an array of large department stores, trendy boutiques and international speciality shops.

The eastern portion of Nanjing Lu is now the **Nanjing Road Pedestrian Mall**, complete with its own electric train serving as a shoppers' shuttle (open daily 9am–9pm; fare for shuttle). Closed to motor traffic since 1999, this 'golden mile' is lined with buildings from Shanghai's colonial past, including its four great department stores: the Hualian Department Store (635 Nanjing Dong Lu), the Shanghai Fashion Company (650 Nanjing Dong Lu), the Shanghai No. 1 Provisions Store (700 Nanjing Dong Lu), and the No. 1 Department Store (800 Nanjing Dong Lu). The No. 1 Department Store, built in 1934, attracts several hundred thousand Chinese shoppers on a good day. Nanjing Road also has a branch of Silk King (66 Nanjing Dong Lu), Shanghai's largest silk and fabric retailer, with clothing on the rack, fabric on the bolt and tailors in the wings.

At Renmin Park, where the pedestrian mall ends, bargain hunters can make a detour below Renmin Square into the **D-Mall** (open daily 10am–9pm). Officially known as the Hong Kong Shopping Centre, this is really a below-ground outdoor market with hundreds of vendors hawking designer-label fashions, cosmetics, shoes and accessories.

The many shops, malls and department stores along **Huaihai Zhong Lu** in the French Concession are generally more upmarket than those on Nanjing Road. Some call Huaihai Zhong Lu the Champs-Elysées of Shanghai – an exaggeration, although this is where Paris-based Sephora opened its first cosmetics store in China (2005). Huaihai Zhong Lu intersects smaller shopping streets such as Maoming Nan Lu and Ruijin Lu, with their fashionable dress shops, clothing boutiques and home décor outlets, and it crosses paths with Hengshan Lu, where the villas have become gift shops and stylish cafés.

Shanghai No. 1 Provisions Store

Shoppers seeking Chinese antiques, teapots, jade, pearls, gold jewellery, fans or walking sticks can find dozens of shops in the **Yuyuan Bazaar**, the pedestrian mall at the heart of Shanghai's Old Town (Nanshi District). The southern border of this bazaar, **Fangbang Zhong Lu**, is itself a prime shopping destination. Remodelled as 'Shanghai Old Street', this avenue is chockablock with antiques and collectibles.

The next wave in Shanghai shopping is gathering momentum along the **Bund**, where two historic buildings have already been tastefully made over into upmarket malls. Three On the Bund (3 Zhongshan Dong Yi Lu), the former Union Insurance Company building, built in 1922, already houses the Evian Spa and Giorgio Armani's flagship store in China. The Bund 18 (18 Zhongshan Dong Yi Lu), the former Chartered Bank of India, Australia and China (1923), became the second Bund building to undergo a modern commercial transformation (in 2005). Its foyer sports a 3-m (10-ft) red chandelier fashioned by Venetian glassmaker Filippo Gabbiani; its shops include Cartier, and its bistro at the rear, the Sibilla Boutique Café, is owned by Italy's Moratti family, which also owns the Serie Aside InterMilan football team.

Shanghai by the Book

Finding books, magazines and newspapers in one's own language has been made more pleasant and convenient with the opening in 2005 of **Garden Books** (325 Chang Le Lu, French Concession; open daily 10am–10pm), an exclusively Western bookshop occupying a stylish two-storey colonial villa. With airy interiors designed by Italian architect Luigi Novelli, Garden Books has an extensive collection of books in many Western languages, as well as a café serving coffee and ice-cream on the first floor and a children's nook upstairs, where a sunroom invites shoppers to linger for hours over a good read.

ENTERTAINMENT

Shanghai's nightlife and its performing-arts scene have both improved rapidly over the past few years, giving travellers more to enjoy here after dark than anywhere else in China, except Hong Kong.

Acrobatics and Opera

The favourite theatrical performances in Shanghai are by its acrobatic troupe, the finest in China. The troupe regularly performs at **Shanghai Circus World** (2266 Gonghexin Lu, Zhabei District; tel: 021 5665 3646), often in tandem with resident circus performers and exotic animals. Acrobats also often headline evenings at the **Shanghai Centre Theatre** (1376 Nanjing Xi Lu, Jingan District; tel: 021 6279 8663).

Inside the Shanghai Concert Hall

Traditional Chinese opera finds appropriate stages on which to perform at the renovated 1920s **Yifu Theatre** (701 Fu Zhou Lu, Renmin Square; tel: 021 6351 4668), the 1930s **Lyceum Theatre** (57 Maoming Nan Lu, French Concession; tel: 021 6217 8530) and the 1940s **Majestic Theatre** (66 Jiang Ning Lu, off Nanjing Xi Lu; tel: 021 6217 4409). Beijing-style opera is most often performed

Theatres have their own box offices, and hotel concierges can sometimes come up with tickets to performances. Otherwise, try the Shanghai Cultural Information and Booking Centre (272 Feng Xian Lu, Jingan District; tel: 021 6217 2426), located north of the Westgate Mall off Nanjing Xi Lu.

by a local Shanghai company at the Yifu Theatre, while Shanghai's own regional styles of Huju and Kunju opera play to smaller local audiences.

International Performances

When international performers of Western classical music visit Shanghai, as they increasingly do, they usually perform at the state-of-the-art **Shanghai Grand Theatre** (300 Renmin Da Dao, Renmin Square; tel: 021 6372 8701; <www.shgtheatre.com>). Shanghai's own world-class symphony orchestra is at home in the 1930s **Shanghai Concert Hall** (523 Yan An Dong Lu, south of Renmin Square; tel: 021 6386 9153). Top Asian and Western rock and pop stars play outdoor stages in city parks or pack the Shanghai Grand Stage in **Shanghai Stadium** (1111 Caoxi Bei Lu, Xuhui District; tel: 021 6438 5200).

Rock, Jazz and Disco

Shanghai's nightlife continues to shine more brightly. Thousands of nightclubs, hundreds of bars and dozens of discos have sprung up overnight in recent years, with most disappearing just as quickly.

Xintiandi (New Heaven and Earth), the upmarket pedestrian mall of renovated 1920s stone-gate architecture, attracts many of Shanghai's richest trendsetters after dark to its swanky bars, dance floors and ARK Live House (Lane 181, Taicang Lu), a top-rated music venue for rock, jazz and pop groups. On the far side of the river, in Pudong, the most comprehensive nightspot is **Pu-J's Entertainment Centre** (Podium 3, Jinmao Tower/Grand Hyatt Hotel, 88 Shi Ji Da Dao, Pudong), where there are separate arenas for live jazz, disco and karaoke.

Maoming Nan Lu in the French Concession south of Huaihai Zhong Lu is lined with crowded discos and stylish bars and lounges, some serving up live jazz and blues in the evenings. Also a hot spot in the French Concession is the **Park 97** complex in Fuxing Park, a Hong Kong venture that includes several bars and a disco. At the western end of the French Concession one finds a more run-down set of night spots along the once-trendy **Julu Lu**, the provocative statuary at its entrance on Hua Shan Lu recently toppled and removed. The youthful collection of café-bars and discos on the nearby, still-trendy Hengshan

Boogie nights

Living it up in Shanghai

Lu is thriving. One of several brand-new café and bar streets lies a block west of the Shanghai Exhibition Hall on Tongren Lu.

Shanghai's Western bars and cafés usually have a short lifespan. Several old-timers (with 10 years considered elderly) are legends in Shanghai's nightlife line-up. These include O'Malley's Irish Pub (42 Tao Jiang Lu), Face (Bldg 4, Ruijin Hotel), Judy's Too (176 Maoming Nan Lu), the Long Bar (1376 Nanjing Xi Lu), Malone's (255 Tongren Lu), the Peace Hotel Old Jazz Bar (20 Nanjing Dong Lu), and Cloud Nine on the 87th floor and Sky Lounge on the 88th floor of the world's tallest hotel, the Grand Hyatt, in Pudong (88 Shi Ji Da Dao).

SPORTS

Many of Shanghai's residents use the city's parks in the early-morning hours to perform the gentle martial art forms of *tai chi* (*tai ji quan*). Foreign visitors can watch and sometimes join in. Best places for 'shadow-boxing' at dawn include the promenades on either side of the Huangpu River, Renmin Park, the renovated Jingan Park and the colonial-era Fuxing Park.

Among other popular participatory sports in Shanghai are bowling (several thousand lanes) and go-karting. The top hotels all have gyms for workouts, courts for tennis and swimming pools for doing laps. A growing number of golf courses can accommodate foreign players, although the prices are quite steep. Hotel desks can usually book a round for you.

Among spectator sports, basketball is popular, particularly since the Shanghai Sharks won the national championship in 2002 with their star Yao Ming (226cm/7ft 6in), who graduated to the NBA in America and has become one of the world's most recognised sports celebrities. Football (soccer) is equally popular; Liverpool played an exhibition match here in 2003. The Shanghai Tennis Masters Cup attracts world stars every September, and the Shanghai International Marathon does likewise in November.

Formula One Grand Prix racing made its China debut in 2004 on a new 14-turn circuit in the Anting District north-west of central Shanghai. This international racing event will be held annually in Shanghai until 2010.

Formula One racing

CHILDREN'S SHANGHAI

In Chinese culture, the family is the central entity, and in Shanghai this translates into an abundance of attractions children can enjoy. The riverfront promenades, for example, are connected by the **Bund Tourist Tunnel** (open daily 9am–9.30pm; admission fee), a fantasy light show under the Huangpu River that employs speedy glass capsules to cover the 647-m (2,123-ft) passageway in a flash.

There are plenty of youth-oriented attractions on the Pudong riverside, beginning with two spectacularly high 360-degree observation decks: one on the **Oriental Pearl TV Tower** *(see page 64)*; the other on the 88-storey **Jin-mao Tower** *(see page 66)*. Northeast of the TV tower is the **Shanghai Ocean Aquarium** (158 Yin Cheng Bei Lu; open daily 9am–9pm; admission fee), one of Asia's largest, with an enormous underwater viewing tunnel 155m (500ft) long surrounded by sharks. Northwest of the TV tower is another childhood wonderland, the **Natural Wild Insect Kingdom** (1 Feng He Lu; open Mon–Fri 9am–5pm, Sat–Sun 9am–5.30pm; admission fee), a hands-on bug-catcher's dream. The interactive **Shanghai Science and Technology Museum** (2000 Shi Ji Da Dao, Pudong; open Tue–Sun 9am–5pm; admission fee) has its own indoor rainforest and two IMAX 3-D cinemas. Pudong's **Century Park** (1001 Jin Xiu Lu; <www.century park.com.cn>; open daily 7am–6pm; admission fee) has plenty of activities, from pedal car and boat hire to miniature golf and a wildlife park.

On the west side of the river, the **Shanghai Zoo** *(see page 60)* is the leading children's attraction, with its pandas, playground, Ferris wheel and bumper cars. **Renmin Square** is the place to buy and fly kites. Dinosaur skeletons and stuffed critters are among the attractions at the old (1956) **Shanghai Natural History Museum** (260 Yan An Dong Lu, west of the lower Bund; open daily 9am–3.30pm; admission fee).

Zhongshan Park (780 Changning Lu; open daily 5am–7pm; admission fee), with its own Metro stop in the Changning District, has a multitude of amusements, from merry-go-rounds to paintball, as well as Fun Dazzle, an immense indoor playground (open daily 9am–5pm, admission fee). Further west is **Aquaria 21** (Gate 4, Changfeng Park; open daily 9am–5pm; admission fee), with a vast underground aquarium, a stadium for viewing Beluga whale shows and supervised scubadiving with the sharks.

Shanghai's premier water park is **Dino Beach**, southwest of the city in the Minhang District (78 Xin Zhen Lu; open daily late June–early Sept 9am–11pm; admission fee), with plenty of slides, rapids and wave pools.

Playtime in the Natural Wild Insect Kingdom

Calendar of Events

The exact dates for Chinese holidays are determined by the lunar calendar; check local listings for times and events.

January–February *Chinese New Year* (2007: 18 Feb; 2008: 7 Feb; 26 Jan 2009), also known as Spring Festival, extends for two weeks, with fireworks, lion dances and special festivities at Longhua Temple. The *Lantern Festival* (15th day after New Year) in Yu Garden marks the end of the New Year celebrations.

March-April *Shanghai International Fashion Culture Festival* – competitions are held at shopping malls in mid-March. *Buddha's Birthday* – celebrated by monks at Jingan Temple.

April *Qing Ming Festival* (5 April; 4 April in leap years) – memorial for the dead, on which hundreds of thousands of people clean ancestral graves. *Longhua Temple Fair* (early April) – 10 days of offerings of food and song. *Nanhui Peach Blossom Festival* (mid-April) – spring festival with folk performances and farm tours.

May *May Day* – covers the first week of the month, when many workers take holidays. The *Shanghai International Music Festival* – concerts by world-class performers.

May–June *Dragon Boat Festival* – colourful boat races are staged on the Huangpu River.

June *Shanghai International Film Festival.*

July *Founding of the Communist Party* (1 July) – marked at its original site, 374 Huangpi Nan Lu. The *Shanghai Beer Festival* (late July) – takes place on the Bund Promenade.

September *Mid-Autumn Festival* – performances in Guilin Park. *Shanghai Grand Prix.*

October *Shanghai Tourism Festival* – a kaleidoscope of cultural events and performances in city parks and shopping locations.

November *Shanghai Marathon.*

November–December *Shanghai International Arts Festival* – a month of blockbuster performances.

31 December *Longhua Bell Festival* – rings in the Western New Year.

EATING OUT

Dining in Shanghai can be as expensive as one likes, although not perhaps as cheap as one would hope. Meals can consist of excellent Shanghai dishes, fine selections from China's other regional cuisines, some top Asian offerings and superb Western renditions by French and French-trained chefs. Meals can also consist of fast food, whether it be Chinese, Japanese, international or pure American. Shanghai does not yet rank as a world-class gourmet destination, but it has made rapid strides in that direction, and finding an elegant restaurant with a menu and wine list to match is not a problem; nor is finding a Chinese restaurant housed in a colonial villa that can satisfy both the palate and the curious eye. Shanghai is international enough so that one can eat a range of dishes in interesting places and be assured of an English-language menu, English-speaking waiter and Western standards of hygiene, although some of the most interesting cafés lack all three.

Dumpling stall

WHERE TO EAT

Until the 1990s, hotel restaurants offered far and away the best dishes in Shanghai, regardless of cuisine or price, but when the free-market reforms kicked in, private restaurants began to take on the big players. Today the field for fine dining is tilted towards a wide range of private restaurants competing against well-established, well-run international hotel spots. Cheaper eats are largely in the hands of café-bars catering to Westerners, fast-food outlets and delis, some private and some in hotels. Street food, prepared by pavement vendors, is still available, particularly at markets, and small local cafés are everywhere, but both require an adventurous spirit, communication skills and a tolerance for smoke and grime.

The finest dining establishments are concentrated in the French Concession, but there are good choices scattered throughout the city on streets that visitors most often frequent. Chinese-style restaurants provide chopsticks (*kwai zi*), although most will happily furnish you with spoons (*shao zi*) and forks (*cha zi*). Dining is casual. Vegetable dishes

Eats in the Streets

Vendors hawking snacks hot off the wok used to be a fixture along Shanghai's side streets, but their kind has become rare in the city centre. Lamb kebabs and flat breads *(nang)* are still sold as they are grilled and fried on Yun Nan Nan Lu at Ning Hai Nan Lu. Card tables set up along Wu Jiang Lu west of Renmin Park off Nanjing Road are filled with crayfish, rice dumplings in palm leaves and beer. Huang He Lu north of the Park Hotel on Nanjing Road specialises in quick, inexpensive skewered meats, bubble teas, pulled noodles and fish balls with seaweed. One of the most diverse and upmarket food streets is Hong Mei Lu Pedestrian Street in Gubei, an expatriate enclave west of the city centre, which features 20 restaurants (rather than stalls), 10 bars and one *mah-jongg* club. The reasonably priced dishes here range from Chinese, Korean and Japanese to American, French and German.

The fast-food option

come first, followed by main dishes, often served communal-style on a single platter. Soup and dessert, usually fresh-fruit slices, come last. Rice, considered a peasant's dish, sometimes requires a special order.

Meal times are often on the early side, with lunch hours 11am–2pm and dinner 5–8pm. Hotel restaurants and many private establishments now take credit cards, but it's best to carry enough local cash to cover the bill. Tipping is not mandatory. Hotel restaurants usually attach a 15 percent service charge to the bill.

WHAT TO EAT

Chinese Cuisine

Chinese dining is made up of a number of regional cuisines, and Shanghai offers an inviting selection of them, beginning with the city's own Shanghainese cuisine. The local specialities are distinguished by rich flavours and textures and brown sauces. The Shanghai version of the popular Cantonese dumplings are steamed in a gelatin mixture and dipped in distinctive brown vinegar, which is also used in stir-fries. Wheat is favoured over rice by the Shanghainese, meaning various kinds of bread are common. Seafood, particularly eel and crab, are signature main dishes, headlined by hairy crab *(da zha xie)*, at its freshest in the autumn. Difficult to crack, it must be prised open and pulled apart with a fork or chopsticks, but waiters can assist the uninitiated. Shanghai has a number of the world's best Shanghainese restaurants, of course, with many housed in old mansions and villas.

Cantonese is the second most popular Chinese cuisine in Shanghai, its origins in south China. Chefs from Hong Kong are regularly recruited to prepare the dishes in Shanghai's pricier Cantonese restaurants. Steaming and stir-frying tend

Shanghainese cuisine: a plate of hairy crabs

to seal in the delicate flavours of the rice noodles, seafood, shark's fin soups and pastries *(dim sum)* that are hallmarks of this cuisine, which is known worldwide.

Sichuan cuisine is celebrated for its spiciness, produced by the use of dried chillies and peppercorns. Hot and sour soup is one of Sichuan's most popular creations. The dishes tend to be

Tucking in to a local delicacy

far hotter in Shanghai than in the West. Hunan cuisine also employs chillies. Dongbei cooking, based on the fare of Beijing and northeast China, is best known for its Peking duck, widely available in Shanghai. The duck is carved into thin slices and rolled in a pancake, seasoned with plum sauce and spring onions. Xinjiang dishes are also a Shanghai favourite, in part a central-Asian cuisine that is marked by its skewers of lamb and flat breads.

International Cuisine

Given its heritage as a cosmopolitan city, it is not surprising to find that Shanghai has flavoured its recent prosperity with a number of outstanding Asian and Western restaurants. Thai is probably the most popular Asian offering, with a half-dozen fine restaurants and cafés in competition for the discriminating foreign diner. Most of Shanghai's top Thai restaurants feature Thai chefs and authentic ingredients. Prices, particularly at lunchtime, can be reasonable. Japanese restaurants are also fairly common in the city, particularly in Gubei New Town to the west and along Huaihai Zhong Lu in the French Concession, areas frequented by

In 2005 McDonald's moved its China headquarters from Hong Kong to Shanghai, from where it planned to launch 100 new Chinese outlets within the year. By 2008 Starbucks intends to have more coffee shops in China than in the US. There are already more Starbucks in Shanghai than in most of the world's large cities.

Shanghai's population of Japanese expatriate workers. Sashimi, yakatori and tempura dishes are available at a wide range of prices, with a number of sushi cafés offering economical lunches. Several Indian and Indonesian restaurants also offer excellent, if not exactly world-class, entrees.

The fiercest competition in Western cuisines takes place at the high-end, led by several world-class French and Continental restaurants newly perched on the Bund and presided over by European master chefs. French and European dining has long been an expensive staple at Shanghai's leading international hotels, where French-trained foreign chefs continue to make their mark. The most stylish of the French-influenced restaurants can also be classified as fusion restaurants, as they constantly blend Chinese and Asian ingredients and approaches with traditional French and nouveau cuisine creations.

Shanghai has a growing number of Western restaurants and cafés that draw upon Italian, German, Irish, English and Mexican cuisines. Leading hotels usually feature a top-flight Western restaurant concentrating on one or more of these traditions, particularly Italian. Less expensive versions have proliferated across the French Concession in the form of stylish villa restaurants and more basic Western-style café-bars.

America's hand is most prominent in the flood of popular chain restaurants and fast-food outlets that crisscross the main shopping and tourist streets. Every block of Nanjing

Road and Huaihai Zhong Lu and every department store and new mall is festooned with Starbucks, McDonald's, Pizza Huts and the like. International delis, often located in major hotel lobbies, such as those at the Hilton and Westin, provide a Western alternative, as do some of the Western bars and cafés in the streets. Check the English-language menus posted on café windows for prices and dishes if the thought of a Shanghai Burger King or a Shanghai Hooters is too much to stomach.

Sunday brunch has become extremely competitive among Shanghai's glittering hotels, with the top choices offering not only a buffet of Western standards, but Chinese and Asian selections, too, along with open kitchens cooking seafood to the customer's satisfaction. Quality champagnes, live entertainment and international promotions also come with these late-morning, early-afternoon repasts. The Westin, Ritz-

Freshly steamed dim sum

Carlton, Grand Hyatt, Four Seasons and Hilton are at the forefront of this culinary fray, with tabs sometimes topping 320 yuan ($40) per customer.

Teahouses

Tea originated in China, where tea-drinking first reached ceremonial heights, and tea remains the most common and preferred beverage among Shanghai residents. Visitors wishing to partake of tea and snacks in a teahouse might start at China's most famous old teahouse, where visiting heads of state have often sat: the Huxinting Teahouse on the lake in the Yuyuan Bazaar *(see page 38)*. Nearby, on 'Shanghai Old Street' (Fangbang Zhong Lu), are several more antiquated tea emporiums, including the Old Shanghai Teahouse (385 Fangbang Zhong Lu; tel: 021 5382 1202; open daily 8.30am–11pm).

Chinese tea as art form

The presence of more than three dozen Starbucks and a spate of Haagen-Dazs ice-cream pavilions has helped reduce the survival rate of traditional teahouses, where Shanghainese once whiled away the hours over a cup of flower tea, although one can still sip the finest Chinese green teas in the old-world atmosphere of Tangyun (119 Hengshan Lu, French Concession), Mingren (9 Duolun Lu, Hongkou District), the Antique Tea Room (1315 Fuxing Lu, French Concession) , the Qiuping Tea House (500 Xiangyang Nan Lu, French Concession), or the Yi He Tea House (158 Hua Yuan Shi Qiao Lu, Pudong). A more cutting-edge, but quite tranquil, tea-drinking experience is offered at Herbal Legend (Unit 1, No. 1, Lane 123, Xing Ye Lu) in Xintiandi, where each of the 10 herbal and fruit teas, served with snacks, promises to work health and beauty miracles.

To Help you Order...

Waiter!/Waitress!	**Fu wu yuan**
Do you have a set menu?	**Tao can?**
I'm a vegetarian.	**Wo shi chi su.**
No MSG, please.	**Qing bu yao fang wei jing.**
The bill, please.	**Qing kai zhang dan.**
I'd like a/an/some...	**Wo xiang you...**
beer	**pi jiu**
bottled water	**kuang quan shui**
cup	**bei zi**
chopsticks	**kuai zi**
coffee	**ka fei**
coke	**ke kou ke le**
fork	**cha zi**
ice	**bing**
knife	**dao zi**
menu	**cai dan**
milk	**niu nai**

salt	**yan**
soda	**qi shui**
spoon	**shao zi**
tea (Chinese)	**cha**
tea (English)	**ying guo cha**
wine	**pu tao jiu**
yoghurt	**suan nai**

....and Read the Menu

Beijing kao ya	Peking duck
chao fan	fried rice
chao huang shan	fried eel
chao shijin sucai	stir-fried vegetables
da zha xie	hairy crab
dou fu	bean curd (tofu)
gong bao ji ding	chicken with peanuts
hong shao shan yu	eel in soy sauce
hundun tang	won ton soup
huo guo	hotpot
ji dan	eggs
jiang zhi qie zi	aubergine (eggplant) in ginger
jiao zi	steamed pastries
mi fan	boiled rice
mian tiao	noodles
qing zheng gui yu	steamed fish
suan la tang	hot and sour soup
tie ban niu rou	beef (sizzling plate)
xiang su ji	crispy chicken
xiao chi	dumplings Shanghai-style
yang rou	lamb
yao guo ji ding	chicken with cashews
youbao xiaren	fried shrimp/prawn
zhu rou	pork
zui ji	drunken (wine-soaked) chicken

HANDY TRAVEL TIPS

An A–Z Summary of Practical Information

A

ACCOMMODATION (see also RECOMMENDED HOTELS, page 129)

Shanghai has many international chain hotels, all at a luxury level (four and five stars by China's official ratings), with prices to match. Book ahead of arrival, particularly from April to October. Hotel websites and internet hotel booking services offer the best room rates.

The major hotels are located in several clusters, including near the river in Pudong, in the centre in the Bund and Nanjing Road sectors, in the French Concession, in the Jingan District northwest of central Shanghai and further west in the Xuhui District. Hotels near Metro stops are the most convenient.

Some Chinese-managed properties, including smaller boutique hotels, are located in historic mansions or villas; these provide adequate services and lower room rates. Generally the international chain hotels offer the highest levels of service, the most amenities, excellent restaurants and the best locations for shopping and sightseeing.

| Single room | **Danren fangjian** | 单人房间 |
| Double room | **Shuangren fangjiān** | 双人房间 |

AIRPORTS

Shanghai has two airports, the old Hongqiao International Airport to the west and the new Pudong International Airport to the east. The Hongqiao facility handles most domestic flights in China, while Pudong International sees almost all international arrivals and departures.

Pudong (tel: 021 3848 4500 ext 2, <www.shairport.com>) is 45km (30 miles) east of the city centre, a 45–90-minute transfer by taxi, hotel shuttle or airport bus. Signs are in English. There are counters for money exchange, city information and hotel reservations in the arrivals hall. Most of the hotels have counters in the arrivals hall, and staff can help arrange transport for guests.

Avoid touts and select a taxi with a meter. Taxis can cost up to 200 yuan ($25), depending on destination. Far less expensive are the official airport buses that serve Pudong International with stops at various major hotels. Check with the airport bus counter for tickets and correct bus number. The Maglev (magnetic levitation) train runs between Pudong International and the Longyang Lu Metro stop on Metro Line 2. If you know your way around the Shanghai Metro system, can afford the ticket on this high-speed connector (30km/19 miles in 8 minutes) and are willing to haul your luggage between some stations, this can be a quick transfer.

Hongqiao (tel: 021 6268 8918 ext 2, <www.shairport.com>) is 19km (12 miles) from the city centre. The recently expanded old airport has money exchange and information counters in its arrivals hall. Hotel desks often provide inexpensive shuttles. Otherwise, the taxi queue is outside; fares run up to 100 yuan ($12.50), depending on destination. Hongqiao Airport has no Metro link yet, and the buses into town are the normal city buses lacking English-language signs and English-speaking drivers.

B

BUDGETING FOR YOUR TRIP

Shanghai is an expensive city, so come prepared with a generous budget. The following are given as a rough guide only:

Accommodation. Double room in an international chain hotel in or near the centre of town, excluding breakfast and 15 percent tax: 800–2,400 yuan ($100–300) per night and up.

Meal and Drinks. Breakfast at a deli or local café-bar, 40–80 yuan ($5–10), or morning buffet in a major hotel, 120–200 yuan ($18–25); set lunch in a local café or hotel restaurant, 50–100 yuan ($6–12); dinner (starter, main course, dessert at a good villa or hotel restaurant),

160–320 yuan ($20–40). Chinese meals can be much cheaper, depending on the number of dishes ordered. A pint of local beer costs as little as 25 yuan ($3); imported beer, as much as 65 yuan ($8); a coffee, 16–25 yuan ($2–3).

Entertainment. A ticket to local performances (such as those by the Shanghai Acrobatic Troupe) costs 50–100 yuan ($6–12); to international performances, 100–600 yuan ($6–72) and up. Museums, art galleries, historic residences and the like generally cost well under 20 yuan ($2.50), although some attractions, such as the Pearl of the Orient TV Tower, can cost as much as 100 yuan ($12.50).

Transport. The Metro costs 2–5 yuan (25–60 cents) per ride, depending on distance travelled. Buses charge 1–2 yuan (12–25 cents) each way. Taxis cost 10 yuan ($1.25) for the first 2km (1¼ miles), 2 yuan (25 cents) for each additional kilometre (0.6 mile), which keeps the fare for most trips around town in the 20 yuan ($2.50) range.

C

CAR HIRE

Tourists do not qualify to drive hire cars, but they can easily hire a car with a qualified local driver. Most hotels provide this service on request, although their price will be steep. Tourists can also hire a car and driver through one of Shanghai's travel agencies or directly from car rental companies such as Hertz (suite 306, Chengfeng Centre, 1088 Yan An Xi Lu, Changning District, tel: 021 6252 2200) or Avis's partner, Shanghai Anji Car Rental (1387 Chang Ning Lu, tel: 021 6268 0862).

CLIMATE

The summers in Shanghai are hot and humid, the winters windy and cold enough for a few snowfalls. September sees some typhoons. October and November are mild months and relatively dry. March and April are also mild, but rainy. Approximate monthly average temperatures are as follows:

	J	F	M	A	M	J	J	A	S	O	N	D
°F	39	41	48	58	68	75	82	82	74	66	54	45
°C	4	5	9	15	20	24	28	28	24	19	12	7

CLOTHING

Shanghai residents are among China's most stylish, but Western tourists do not have to keep up. Sporty casual wear is fine, supplemented by comfortable, study walking shoes. An umbrella, raincoat and light sweater or jacket offer enough protection, except during the cold temperatures of winter months.

Very few of even Shanghai's top restaurants post dress codes. Suits are not worth packing, although sports coats are widely worn by residents and working expats. Shorts, slip-on sandals and skimpy summer wear have not caught on in the city's streets, except on the very hottest days.

COMPLAINTS

It's 'buyer beware' in Shanghai, where very few independent merchants are willing to refund a purchase, whatever the reason. In theory, consumers can complain to the Shanghai Bureau of Quality and Technical Supervision (<www.sbts.sh.cn>), but language problems and bureaucratic shuffling seldom lead to a satisfactory outcome. Some department stores and malls maintain effective complaint desks, and taxi service complaints can be lodged by phone (tel: 021 6323 2150).

CRIME AND SAFETY

As the city modernises, its urban crime rates increase as well, but Shanghai is safer than most big cities overseas. Thieves and pick-pockets sometimes target Western tourists. Markets, the Metro, crowded streets and tourist sites are among places a visitor must keep valuables concealed inside, not outside, clothing.

Although it is sometimes tempting, do not extend conversations with strangers or go to places off the beaten track with 'friends' practising a little English who come up to you in the streets, as money is the overwhelming motive for such encounters. Shanghai has hundreds of con-artists of every description working the city, with some specialising in removing cash from foreign travellers.

In an emergency, dial 110 for the police and ask for an English-speaking officer.

Call the police!	**jiao jing cha**
Help!	**jiu-ren a**
Call a doctor!	**qi sheng**
Danger!	**wei-xian**

CUSTOMS AND ENTRY REQUIREMENTS

All travellers to China must have a passport that is valid upon arrival for at least six months thereafter (with two blank pages remaining) and a visa that is approved and stamped into the passport at a Chinese embassy or consulate before departure to China. The first step is to determine the location and visa policies of the nearest Chinese embassy or consulate. Contact information worldwide can be found on the official website of the Chinese Ministry of Foreign Affairs (<www.fmprc.gov.cn/eng>). Some consulates require visa registration in person, some by post, and the process usually involves filling out a simple form and enclosing a passport photo, along with the current application fee. It is prudent to start the visa application process at least 90 days before you travel. Most tourists apply for a single-entry 'L' visa that begins on the day of actual entry into

China and is good for 30 days. An increasing number of private travel agencies in North America and Europe will take care of the visa paperwork and sometimes expedite it for China travellers, all at an extra fee.

Chinese customs allows each visitor to bring in three cartons of cigarettes, four bottles (0.75 litres each) of alcoholic beverages, and electronic items for personal use including cameras, video recorders and portable (laptop) computers. Items prohibited from entry include animals, drugs, firearms, plant material and media in any form deemed 'detrimental' to China's social and political well-being, such as pornography or religious works.

Note that no one can take out of China any purchased antique item created before 1795, and that antiques made in China from 1795 to 1949 must have an official red wax seal to be allowed out of the country.

E

ELECTRICITY

Electricity is 220-volt, alternating current (AC), 50 cycles. Transformers may be required to operate certain electronic devices, including laptops and mobile phone chargers. Outlets in China come in four main configurations: flat two-pin, round two-pin, slanted two-prong and slanted three-prong. Hotels usually can lend outlet adapters to guests.

EMBASSIES AND CONSULATES

The consulates listed below, located in the Jingan District and the French Concession, are not open on weekends and sometimes close for lunch (1–2pm).

Australia 22nd Floor, CITIC Square, 1168 Nanjing Xi Lu, tel: 021 5292 5500, <www.china.embassy.gov.au/shanghai>.

Canada Suite 604, Shanghai Centre, 1376 Nanjing Xi Lu, tel: 021 6279 8400, <www.shanghai.gc.ca>.
Ireland Room 700A, Shanghai Centre, 1376 Nanjing Xi Lu, tel: 021 6279 8729, <www.foreignaffairs.gov.ie/irishembassy/China.htm>.
New Zealand Room 1605–1607A, The Centre, 989 Chang Le Lu, tel: 021 5407 5858, <www.nzembassy.com>.
UK Suite 301, Shanghai Centre, 1376 Nanjing Xi Lu, tel: 021 6279 7650, <www.uk.cn>.
USA 1469 Huaihai Zhong Lu, tel: 021 6433 6880, <www.usembassy-china.org.cn/shanghai>.

Embassy	**Dashiguan**	大使馆
Passport	**Huzhao**	护照
Visa	**Qianzheng**	签证

EMERGENCIES

For police, dial 110. For fire services, dial 119. For ambulance, dial 120. Only the police emergency number can provide an English-speaking operator.

G

GAY AND LESBIAN TRAVELLERS

Shanghai lacks an organised gay scene, but the latest gossip from gay Shanghai can be accessed online at <www.utopia-asia.com>. Many leading restaurants have a gay-friendly reputation, as do some of the public bathhouses and fitness clubs, and overt discrimination against homosexuals, particularly foreigners, is practically unheard of – but the gay community is nearly invisible, too. There are often around a dozen nightspots favoured by gays and lesbians in the city, but their longevity and location are unpredictable. Internet listings and bar listings in Shanghai magazines can help in locating current hot spots. Even Eddy's, the longest-running gay bar, has moved a half-dozen times in the past decade.

GETTING TO SHANGHAI

By Air. Regular daily flights connect Shanghai's Pudong International Airport with most of the world's major airports. China's own air carriers are the only airlines allowed to connect Shanghai with the rest of China, doing so from the Hongqiao Airport, usually with daily or twice-daily flights on up-to-date aircraft.

By Train. Passengers arriving by overnight train from Hong Kong undergo customs and immigration procedures before departing. Train passengers from elsewhere in China need only show their ticket upon arrival. The main train from Hong Kong takes 29 hours and provides sleeping compartments and a dining service. Shanghai Railway Station (tel: 021 6354 3193 or 021 6317 9090) is near the Metro Line 1 station of the same name, north of central Shanghai in the Zhabei District.

| Airport | **Feijichang** | 飞机场 |
| Railway station | **Huoche zhan** | 火车站 |

GUIDED TOURS

Day tours. Many Shanghai hotel desks can reliably arrange day tours of the city or spots of particular interest for their guests. An English-speaking guide and local driver conduct visitors from site to site, pausing for lunch in a Chinese restaurant. When a day tour is booked through a major hotel by just one or two travellers, it can be quite rewarding, but expensive, as these tours are priced based on the number of participants. When time is of the essence, however, a day tour is the answer. Many hotels depend on the services of the city's largest, government-run foreign tourist company, China International Travel

Service (CITS; 1277 Beijing Xi Lu, Jingan District, tel: 021 6289 4510 or 021 6289 8899; or 2 Jingling Dong Lu, Huangpu District, tel: 021 6323 8770, <www.scits.com/eng/default.asp>), and visitors can go directly to these CITS offices to arrange tours, too, but the prices and tours are equivalent to hotel-arranged tours.

Group tours are a cheaper alternative. These are bus tours that also employ one English-speaking guide and one local driver, but accommodate five to 10 times as many visitors, meaning they are more rushed and cursory. They do offer a quick overview of the city's main sights, as well as a basic local lunch. The most experienced operator of group tours in Shanghai is the Jin Jiang Optional Tours Center (161 Chang Le Lu, Jingan District, tel: 021 6415 1188 ext 80160), which also arranges day tours to outlying attractions, hiring of guides, hotel reservations, airport transfers, theatre tickets and river cruises.

River tours. Seeing Shanghai from the river that has powered much of its history and trade can be exhilarating. The Huangpu River Cruise Company (219 Zhongshan Dong Er Lu, tel: 021 6374 4461) provides one-hour round-trip cruises down to the Yangpu Bridge and three-and-a-half-hour cruises all the way to the Yangzi River and back. Tickets and current timetables are available at the company's office on Jingling Pier at the south end of the Bund Promenade. A 30-minute cruise for those in a hurry is also offered from the Pudong side at the dock on Feng He Lu on the northwest side of the Oriental Pearl TV Tower (where tickets can be purchased at the tower's box office).

H

HEALTH AND MEDICAL CARE

China does not have a health-care agreement with any other nation. Some clinics accept private international health insurance, so check before departure. No vaccinations are required for entrance to China, but keep your inoculations up to date. Consult the World Health Organisation (<www.who.int/en>) for current warnings. Bring your regular medications and prescriptions with you and do not drink tap water.

Shanghai has the most advanced medical system in China. Major hospitals and clinics treating foreigners (with Western-style medicine) include World Link Medical and Dental Centers (Suite 203, Shanghai Centre, 1376 Nanjing Xi Lu, tel: 021 6279 7688, <www.worldlink-shanghai.com>), with 24-hour emergency services and Western dental care. Major hotels usually maintain a small clinic, have doctors on-call and can refer a guest to a doctor or clinic for treatment.

Late pharmacy: 24-hour daily service at Huaihai Pharmacist (528 Huaihai Zhong Lu at Chongqing Nan Lu, tel: 021 6372 2101).

As Shanghai's middle class grows, so does its pet population, but the only champion of abandoned and injured dogs and cats is the recently formed Shanghai Small Animal Protection Association (tel: 138 1781 1443; email: <petsunion@yahoo.com.cn>).

Pharmacy	**Yaodian**	药店
Hospital	**Yiyuan**	医院
Doctor	**Daifu/yisheng**	大夫/医生

L

LANGUAGE

The official language of the People's Republic of China is *putonghua*, roughly the form of the language spoken in Beijing, which is also known as Mandarin. Shanghai natives speak their own distinct dialect, Shanghainese, difficult for even Mandarin speakers to understand. Regardless of dialect, Chinese speakers share a written language in common, consisting of Chinese characters, of which about 5,000 are in common daily use.

The sound of each character as spoken in the standard (Mandarin) dialect has been rendered into a Romanised system called *pinyin*, which employs letters from the alphabet to mimic the sounds and carry the meaning of Chinese words. Pronouncing *pinyin* has its own nuances and complications. Among the biggest stumbling blocks are the following consonants (accompanied by approximate English equivalents).

c	like ts in the word '**its**'
g	hard g as in '**g**ive'
h	like ch in Scottish 'lo**ch**'
j	like j in '**j**eer'
q	similar to ch in '**ch**eer'
x	like sh in '**sh**ip'
z	like ds in 'ki**ds**'
zh	like j in '**j**ug'

Most Chinese people know only a few standard phrases of English, and conversations can become painfully stilted. Hotel and airline employees and others who deal with foreigners have usually learnt enough English to cope with everyday problems. Tour guides are trained to specialise in one or more foreign languages, but not all of them have a firm grasp of English. To make yourself understood, you might need to speak slowly, clearly and simply.

Some useful words:

Hello	**ni hao**	Wrong	**bu dui**
Goodbye	**zai jian**	Today	**jin tian**
Thanks	**xie xie**	Tomorrow	**ming tian**
Sorry	**dui bu qi**	Airport	**fei ji chang**
No problem	**mei wen ti**	Metro	**di tie zhan**
It doesn't	**mei**	Taxi	**chu zu qi che**
matter	**guan xi**	OK	**OK**

Some useful questions and answers:

What is this called?	**Zhe jiao shen me ming zi?**
I don't understand	**Wo bu dong**
I don't know	**Wo bu zhi dao.**
What is your name?	**Nin gui xing?**
My name is —	**Wo xing —**
Where are you from?	**Ni shi cong nar lai de?**
I'm from —	**Wo shi — ai de**
England **Ying guo**	USA **Mei guo**
Scotland **Su ge lan**	Canada **Jia na da**
Wales **Wei er shi**	Australia **Ao da li ya**
Ireland **Ai er lan**	New Zealand **Xin xi lan**

For shopping:

How much is this?	**Duo shao qian?**
Too expensive	**tai gui le**
Cheaper?	**pian yi dian?**
Too big/too small	**tai da/tai xiao**
Receipt please	**qing gei wo fa pio**
I want	**wo yao**
Don't want	**bu yao**

Directions:

Road	**lu**	East	**dong**
Street	**xie**	West	**xi**
North	**bei**	Middle	**zhong**
South	**nan**	1/2/3	**yi/er/san**

In the Shanghainese dialect:

Hello	**nong hao**	How much is this?	**Ji di?**
Thank you	**xia xia nong**	Too expensive	**ta ju le**
Taxi	**tsa tou**		

LEFT LUGGAGE

Hotels can arrange short- or long-term luggage storage for guests. There are luggage storage counters at Shanghai Railway Station and the two airports, where rates top 100 yuan ($12.50) per day.

LOST PROPERTY

Property lost in Pudong International Airport can be reported by telephone (tel: 021 6834 6324). Property left in taxis should be reported to the relevant taxi company. Hotel concierges can help in the search. Missing passports should be reported immediately to your consulate.

M

MAPS

Free maps are available at hotel desks. Bookshops and kiosks sell city maps. The most useful map has street names printed in English, *pinyin* (romanised Chinese) and Chinese characters.

MEDIA

Newspapers. The English-language *Shanghai Daily* comes out daily except on Sundays, and it is free.

Listings magazines. Free English-language publications include articles about the city as well as current entertainment and dining lists. Top choices are *8 days*, *That's Shanghai*, *City Weekend*, *Shanghai Talk* and *Quo*.

Television. Major hotels usually have international satellite stations such as CNN, BBC and the Asian version of HBO. Shanghai has an array of local stations, with an occasional programme in English on the SBN station. One of China's national channels, CCTV-9, offers programmes and news in English.

Radio. BBC World Service (<www.bbc.co.uk>) and the Voice of America (<www.voa.gov>) can both be heard on a number of short-wave bands in Shanghai.

MONEY

Currency. The monetary unit is the yuan, also referred to as renminbi (RMB) or kuai, and divided into 10 jiao (or mao). Banknotes: 1 yuan, 2 yuan, 5 yuan, 10 yuan, 20 yuan, 50 yuan, 100 yuan. Coins: 10 jiao, 20 jiao, 50 jiao, 1 yuan.

Banks. China's central bank sets the official exchange rate through the Bank of China. The Bank of China has four convenient branches offering both cash withdrawals using a credit card and currency exchange facilities. They are on the Bund (23 Zhongshan Dong Yi Lu), near the Shanghai JC Mandarin Hotel (1221 Nanjing Xi Lu), at 1207 Huaihai Zhong Lu and at 2168 Yan An Xi Lu. Bank of China hours are Mon–Fri 9am–noon, 1.30–4.30pm, and Sat 9am–noon. Citibank (19 Zhongshan Dong Yi Lu, tel: 021 6329 8383) in the Peace Hotel on the Bund exchanges US currency and American Express US dollar traveller's cheques.

ATMs. Many of these automated cash machines around town cannot handle transactions on international credit cards, but those at Bank of China branches are usually reliable if you have your PIN number, as are the ATMs at the City Supermarket in Shanghai Centre (1376 Nanjing Xi Lu), the Citibank ATM at the Peace Hotel on the Bund and ATMs in major hotels and some shopping malls.

Credit cards. International credit cards are accepted at major hotels, some luxury restaurants and a handful of upmarket shops and malls. Cash advances are available at Bank of China branches; a 4 percent fee is exacted. American Express card holders can enquire about currency exchange, card replacement and cheque cashing at the office in Shanghai Centre (Room 206, 1376 Nanjing Xi Lu, tel: 021 6279 8082; Mon–Fri 9am–5.30pm).

Currency exchange. Exchanging foreign currency is legal only at banks, hotels and some shopping outlets. There are no private exchange services, and the rates at hotels differ little from those at banks. Bank of China branches perform currency exchange, but most travellers rely on their hotel desks.

Traveller's cheque	**Luxing zhipiao**	旅行支票
Credit card	**Xinyongka**	信用卡
Foreign currency	**Waihuiquan**	外汇券

O

OPENING HOURS

Banks. Usually Mon–Fri 9.30am–4.30pm. Some open for limited services on Saturday morning.

Shops. Hours vary. Most shops are open daily 9.30am–9pm. Department stores and malls, 10am–10pm.

Offices. Mon–Fri 9am–5pm. Some close for lunch, noon–1.30pm.

Museums. Usually open seven days a week 9.30am–4pm, although a number of museums and other tourist sights are closed for one day each week.

Bars. Bars that double as cafés often open as early as 7.30am and stay open all day. Others open by noon. The official closing hour is 2am daily.

P

POLICE

Police wear dark navy uniforms. Few speak any foreign language. Traffic guards corral pedestrians at most major intersections. Police stations are marked by a red light and a sign in *pinyin* reading JINGCHA. The main police station of the city's Public Security Bureau (Gong An Ju) is at 210 Hankou Lu. Tel: 021 6357 6666 for an English-speaking officer or 110 for an emergency.

POST OFFICES

Shanghai's main post office (open daily 7am–10pm) is at 276 Bei Suzhou Lu, north of the Bund at Sichuan Bei Lu. There is a branch with English-speaking staff at Shanghai Centre (1376 Nanjing Xi Lu).

International postcards cost 4.2 yuan (about 50 cents). Letters under 20g (0.7oz) to Australia, North America and Europe cost 6.5 yuan (80 cents).

Air mail	**Hangkong xin**	航空信
Postage stamp	**Youpiao**	邮票
Post office	**Youju**	邮局

PUBLIC HOLIDAYS

On the following national holidays, banks and offices are closed, as are some shops, restaurants and tourist sights. These are peak domestic travel periods.

1 January	New Year's Day
January–February	Chinese New Year/Spring Festival (follows the lunar calendar: 18 February 2007; 7 February 2008; 26 January 2009)
1 May	Labour Day
1 October	National Day

PUBLIC TRANSPORT

Metro. There are three Metro lines in Shanghai. Metro Line 1 runs south from Shanghai Railway Station through Renmin Square, across the French Concession along Huaihai Zhong Lu and down Hengshan Lu through the Xuhui District to Shanghai Stadium and the southern suburbs. Metro Line 2 runs from the Maglev high-speed link to Pudong International Airport at Longyang Station northwest through Pudong, crosses the Huangpu River and continues due west along Nanjing Road (from the Bund through Renmin Square to Jingan) and terminates at Zhongshan Park. Metro Line 3 (the elevated Pearl Line) makes an arc on the west side of the city, connecting Shanghai Railway Station in the north to Shanghai Stadium in the south. Line 1 runs north–south, Line 2 east–west through the city. The two lines connect at the main transfer point, Renmin Square, making it a quick matter to get around most of Shanghai, including Pudong.

The clean, modern trains run frequently 5.30am–11pm daily and are often crowded. Avoid rush hours. There is plenty of English-language and *pinyin* signage on Metro maps in the stations and carriages, as well as recorded announcements when under way, making navigation easy.

Ticket machines and manned counters sell individual tickets. Fares depend on destination (check the simple fare maps, usually posted on ticket machines). Single-journey tickets cost 2–5 yuan (25–60 cents). Use the magnetic ticket to enter the turnstile, then retrieve the ticket and use it to exit the turnstile at your destination. Stored-value cards (*jiaotong*), good on the Metro, bus system and even taxis, can be purchased in various amounts at the large service counters in most Metro stations.

Buses. Public buses are slow, crowded and difficult to use (Chinese language only), although they are good value at 1–2 yuan (12–24 cents) per ride.

Ferries and tunnel. To cross the Huangpu River dividing central Shanghai from the new Pudong area, most travellers rely on taxis or the Metro. A cheap alternative is by public ferry, an open-boat affair that connects the south Bund with the Riverside Promenade in Pudong at Dong Chang Lu, all for a 2-yuan (25-cent) ticket. The more expensive crossing is via the Bund Sight-Seeing Tunnel's subterranean tramcars, a tourist attraction in itself (20 yuan/$2.50 one-way; children half-price).

Taxis. Most of Shanghai's 42,000 taxis are new, clean, air-conditioned and efficient, and most drivers are honest. All taxis are required to run the meter and give printed receipts. Expatriates prefer taxis to the Metro for getting around town, as taxis are neither crowded nor costly, although traffic conditions can cause delays.

Trips around the central-city districts seldom cost more than 30 yuan ($3.75). Some taxis are equipped to accept major international credit cards. Very small tips are acceptable, but not expected. The most reliable and comfortable fleets are those of Da Zhong Taxi (tel: 021 6258 1688), Qiang Sheng Taxi (tel: 021 6258 0000) and Jin Jiang Taxi (tel: 021 6275 8800). Taxis may be hailed at major intersections, attractions, marked taxi ranks and hotel entrances.

Bus	**Gong gong qi che**	公共汽车
Taxi	**Chu zu qi che**	出租汽车
Metro	**Di tie zhan**	

T

TELEPHONES

Shanghai's China dialling code is 021. To call from abroad, dial the 86 international code for the People's Republic of China, then 21, then the eight-digit number. To phone abroad from Shanghai, dial 00 followed by the international code for the country you want, then the number: Australia (61), Canada and US (1), Ireland (353), New

Zealand (64), UK (44), etc. If using a phone credit card, first dial the company's access number as follows: AT&T: 10 811; MCI: 10 812; Sprint: 10813.

Mobile phones (cell phones) seem to be in every hand in the streets of Shanghai. They function on the GSM network, as in Europe. Roaming and international charges are high, so purchase of a prepaid SIM card (sold at department stores and newsstands) is recommended. Mobile-phone hire is available at hotel business centres. Public telephone boxes are common in the city; they require a 1 yuan coin or use of a prepaid IC card (sold at post offices and convenience stores).

Operator	**114**
International operator	**116**

Telephone	**Diànhuà**	电话
Long-distance call	**Chángtú diànhuà**	长途电话
International call	**Guójì diànhuà**	国际电话

TIME ZONES

The whole of China follows the same standard time, and does not convert to daylight saving time, so the whole country is at GMT + 8 year-round. For the exact current time in Shanghai, dial 117. The following chart shows time differences in the northern hemisphere winter:

Los Angeles	New York	London	**Shanghai**	Sydney
4am	7am	noon	**8pm**	10pm

TIPPING

Tipping is not legal in China, but nonetheless common practice in Shanghai for bellhops, maids, tour guides and tour bus drivers. A 15 percent service charge is often added to bills at high-quality restaurants.

TOILETS

Public facilities are not always up to Western hygienic standards, and some still offer only the squat toilet, but those that charge a small fee are likely to have Western-style facilities as well as toilet paper. Hotels, department stores and many cafés and restaurants provide better facilities. Signs are posted across the central city indicating the location of nearby public toilets, but always carry tissues and personal hygiene products in case services prove primitive. The city has posted a digital map of nearly 2,000 public toilets in central Shanghai with hours and addresses, but the website is slow to load and in Chinese (<www.sh1111.gov.cn>).

Toilet	**Cesuo**	厕所

TOURIST INFORMATION

The Tourist Information Service Centres in Shanghai are seldom useful to foreign travellers, although there is sometimes a helpful English-speaking clerk on duty, and printed maps and brochures are sometimes available. The main information centre is in Room 410, 2525 Zhongshan Xi Lu (<www.shanghaitour.net>), with branches at 1699 Nanjing Xi Lu, 561 Nanjing Dong Lu, 127 Chengdu Nan Lu and 168 Lujiazui Xi Lu in Pudong. The tourist hotline is sometimes manned by English-speaking operators (tel: 021 6252 0000 or 021 6439 8947), but hotel concierges, guidebooks and local tourist magazines are better sources of information.

Overseas, the China National Tourist Office (CNTO, <www.cnto.org>) provides travel information through branches in several countries:

Australia: China National Tourist Office, 19th floor, 44 Market Street, Sydney NSW 2000, tel: (02) 9299 4057, fax: (02) 9290 1958.
Canada: China National Tourist Office, 480 University Avenue, Toronto, Ontario, M5G 1V2, tel: (416) 599-6636, fax: (416) 599-6382.

UK: China National Tourist Office, 4 Glentworth Street, London NW1 5PG, tel: (020) 7935 9787, fax: (020) 7487 5842.
USA: China National Tourist Office, 350 5th Avenue, Suite 6413, New York, NY 10118, tel: (212) 760-9700, fax: (212) 760 8809.

TRAVELLERS WITH DISABILITIES

In 2004 Shanghai constructed 735km (450 miles) of pavement with a raised circle pattern for the sight-impaired, and 4,000 wheelchair ramps. In 2005 Shanghai became a model non-barrier city in recognition of its progress in building and maintaining facilities for the handicapped. Yet the disabled still confront many obstacles, and this is still a city of long stairways and very few lifts and escalators where they are most needed (such as at the Metro entrances). The situation should improve as Shanghai prepares to host the Special Olympics in 2007. Information is offered through Able-Access Travel Source (<www.access-able.com>) and the Shanghai Disabled Persons' Federation (189 Long Yang Lu, Pudong, tel: 021 5873 3212).

W

WEBSITES AND INTERNET CAFÉS

Most hotels catering to foreign guests provide internet access at PCs in their business centres (40–80 yuan/$5–10 for 10 minutes online), and upmarket hotels offer in-room or Wi-Fi (wireless) connections for guests with portable devices, such as laptops, with varying fees. Top restaurants and malls are beginning to create Wi-Fi zones. Internet cafés include the icafe (Central Plaza, 381 Huaihai Zhong Lu, tel: 021 6391 5582) and the Shanghai Library (1555 Huaihai Zhong Lu, tel: 021 6445 5555). The library is open daily 8.30am–8.30pm and offers the cheapest (8 yuan/$1 per hour) and often most crowded access on its PCs.

For current travel information on Shanghai, popular websites include <www.8days.sh>, <www.thatssh.com>, <www.shanghaitour.net>, <www.cityweekend.com.cn> and <www.shangai-ed.com>.

Recommended Hotels

Travellers preferring a measure of luxury and good service with atten-tive English-speaking staff should select a four- or five-star hotel (as rated by the Chinese Government), which includes the major inter-national chains. Three-star hotels are locally owned and Chinese-managed, with more basic but clean and modern rooms, and fewer facilities. Two-star hotels are favoured by independent travellers seeking spartan but economical lodging. Shanghai has accommoda-tion in each category, with some moderately priced boutique hotels beginning to appear in remodelled colonial villas and mansions.

Reservations are necessary from April to October. Rooms can be booked on the internet, often at a substantial saving, or through toll-free hotel reservation services. Hotels seldom include breakfast or airport transfers in their rates, so enquire ahead about both. Most accept international credit cards, and a 15 percent tax is levied on top of the room rates listed below. Price guides are for a standard double room at full rate. Winter rates (Dec–Feb) are lower.

$$$$$	over 2,000 yuan ($250)
$$$$	1,400–2,000 yuan ($175–250)
$$$	800–1,400 yuan ($100–175)
$$	400–800 yuan ($50–100)
$	under 400 yuan ($50)

HUANGPU (CENTRAL SHANGHAI)

88 Xintiandi $$$$ *380 Huangpi Nan Lu, tel: 021 5383 8833, fax: 021 5383 8877, <www.88xintiandi.com>.* This new Art Deco guest-house in the Xintiandi complex is a favourite of business people who travel in style and want to be close to the upmarket nightlife scene.

Captain's Hostel $ *37 Fuzhou Lu, tel: 021 6323 5053, fax: 021 6321 9331, <www.captainhostel.com.cn>.* Double rooms here are basic and clean with air conditioning, TV and internet access in the lobby. The hostel also has low-cost dormitory beds, bicycle hire and a self-service laundry.

Howard Johnson Plaza Hotel $$$$ *595 Jiujiang Lu, tel: 021 3313 4888, fax: 021 3313 4880, <www.hojochina.com>.* Just south of Nanjing Road and Century Square, Howard Johnson opened this 27-storey tower in 2003; with large rooms, a central location and aspirations to compete with Shanghai's top luxury hotels.

JW Marriott Hotel $$$$$ *399 Nanjing Xi Li, tel: 021 5359 4969, fax: 021 6375 5988, <www.marriotthotels.com/shajw>.* Perched on floors 38–60 of the rocket ship-shaped tower on Tomorrow Square, this super-deluxe, futuristic hotel boasts large rooms, high-tech appliances and fine views over Renmin Square.

Peace Hotel $$$$ *20 Nanjing Dong Lu, tel: 021 6321 6888, fax: 021 6329 0300, <www.shanghaipeacehotel.com>.* Although overpriced and overrated at five stars, the Peace Hotel, built in 1929 as the Cathay Hotel by taipan Victor Sassoon, is an institution. Its Art-Deco architecture has no peer in Shanghai, its Bund location is superb and its restaurants and bars have a definite 1920s atmosphere, too.

Ramada Plaza Shanghai $$$ *700 Jiu Jiang Lu, tel: 021 6350 0000, fax: 021 6350 8490, <www.ramadahotels.com>.* Located right in the heart of the busy Nanjing Road Pedestrian Mall, this modern hotel with an over-the-top European lobby has improved its services and now offers some of the lowest rates on four-star rooms.

Sofitel Hyland Hotel $$$$ *505 Nanjing Dong Lu, tel: 021 6351 5888, fax: 021 6351 7466, <www.accorhotels.com>.* Accor-managed in a rather no-nonsense French manner, the Sofitel has secured a superb location on the Nanjing Road Pedestrian Mall. The compact rooms were renovated in 1998.

The Westin Shanghai $$$$$ *88 Henan Zhong Lu, tel: 021 6335 1888, fax: 021 6335 2888, <www.westin.com>.* The high-end choice in the Bund area, the towering Westin with its blue-glass spiralling staircase combines excellent Western-style services with spacious rooms, plush beds and walk-in 'rainforest' showers. The lobby connects to a smart deli and a Rolls-Royce showroom.

YMCA Hotel $$ *123 Xizang Nan Lu, tel: 021 6326 1040, fax: 021 6320 1957, <www.ymcahotel.com>*. A low-priced option with a good location southwest of Renmin Square, this locally managed backpackers' favourite in the historic 1929 YMCA building gets so-so marks for its rooms and staff.

LUWAN (FRENCH CONCESSION)

Jin Jiang Hotel $$$$ *59 Maoming Nan Lu, tel: 021 6258 2582, fax: 021 6472 5588*. A historic 1929 hotel managed by Shanghai's ubiquitous Jin Jiang Group. The Jin Jiang has a number of structures, including the remodelled North Building. Worth considering for its central French Concession location rather than its service or rates.

Okura Garden Hotel $$$$$ *58 Maoming Nan Lu, tel: 021 6415 1111, fax: 021 6415 8866, <www.gardenhotelshanghai.com>*. Geared to upmarket Japanese travellers in particular, the Garden is a grand complex offering meticulous service while preserving the 1926 ballroom and foyers of the Cercle Sportif French Club.

Ruijin Hotel $$$ *118 Ruijin Er Lu, tel: 021 6472 5222, fax: 021 6473 2277, <www.shedi.net.cn/outEDI/Ruijin>*. Located on the 1930s Morris Estate, this stylish villa complex captures the colonial Shanghai atmosphere, with passable services in keeping with fairly moderate room rates.

JINGAN (NORTHWEST SHANGHAI)

Four Seasons Hotel Shanghai $$$$$ *500 Weihai Lu, tel: 021 6256 8888, fax: 021 6256 5678, <www.fourseasons.com/shanghai>*. Dedicated to luxury, Four Seasons has entered the Shanghai market with a new lavishly furnished tower equipped with 24-hour butler service for each guest and an attentive staff.

Hengshan Moller Villa $$$$ *30 Shaanxi Nan Lu, tel: 021 6247 8881, fax: 021 6289 1020, <www.mollervilla.com>.* A veritable Gothic cathedral among colonial villas, the Moller house has recently opened its doors and gingerbread interiors to guests, who can stay in the overpriced baroque-style rooms in the original 1936 mansion or in the dull new annexe behind for a bit less.

Hilton Hotel $$$$ *250 Huashan Lu, tel: 021 6248 0000, fax: 021 6248 3848, <www.shanghai.hilton.com>.* Foreign-owned and managed since 1987, this is Shanghai's premier deluxe business hotel, with a busy lobby, big new spa, efficient business centre and one of the city's most experienced staffs. Recent room renovations put the Hilton on a par with Shanghai's other top hotels.

Hotel Equatorial $$$$ *65 Yan An Xi Lu, tel: 021 6248 1688, fax: 021 6248 1773, <www.equatorial.com>.* Right next door to the Hilton, with one star less for a bit less service and fewer amenities, the Equatorial is Singapore-managed and attracts guests as much from Southeast Asia as the West.

Old House Inn $$ *No. 16, Lane 351, Huashan Lu, tel: 021 6248 6118, fax: 021 6249 6869, <www.oldhouse.cn>.* A true boutique hotel in the shadow of the Hilton: a dozen rooms, wooden floors, courtyard garden, traditional furniture and a stylish café. Sophisticated, high-value lodging – rare in Shanghai.

Portman Ritz-Carlton Hotel $$$$$ *1376 Nanjing Xi Lu, tel: 021 6279 8888, fax: 021 6279 8800, <www.ritzcarlton.com>.* Northwest Shanghai's top address for more than a decade, this deluxe complex inside the Shanghai Centre puts visitors in touch with every Western amenity imaginable, from Starbucks to a supermarket. Service matches the deluxe guest rooms.

Shanghai JC Mandarin Hotel $$$$ *1225 Nanjing Xi Lu, tel: 021 6279 1888, fax: 021 6279 1314, <www.jcmandarin.com>.* Asian tour groups are attracted by the Singapore management and modern hotel tower, but many Westerners stay here, too. Renovated in 2002, the JC Mandarin has large guest rooms and a children's play area.

XUHUI (SOUTHWEST SHANGHAI)

Regal International East Asia Hotel $$$$$ *516 Hengshan Lu, tel: 021 6415 5588, fax: 021 6445 8899, <www.regal-eastasia. com>*. International management keeps this modern luxury hotel busy. Conveniently located for shopping and eating on Hengshan Lu, the hotel has Shanghai's best tennis facilities.

Shanghai Conservatory of Music Guest House $ *20 Feng Yang Lu, tel: 021 6437 2577, fax: 021 6437 2577*. Of the dorms and doubles with shared baths on this idyllic campus, those in the colonial-era Experts Building, complete with balconies, are most desirable and quite cheap. Wake up to live music.

Taiyuan Villa $$$ *160 Tai Yuan Lu, tel: 021 6471 6688, fax: 021 6471 2618*. This 1920s French colonial mansion was home to US General George Marshall during World War II and to Chairman Mao's wife, Jiang Qing, during the Cultural Revolution. It is now a quiet, comfortable, renovated 19-room retreat with its own garden grounds.

CHANGNING (HONGQIAO DEVELOPMENT ZONE)

Radisson Plaza Xing Guo Hotel $$$$ *78 Xing Guo Lu, tel: 021 6212 9998, fax: 021 6212 9996, <www.radisson.com>*. In 2002 Radisson built a deluxe hotel tower on a colonial garden estate that had served as a Chinese-run hotel for decades. There are rooms available in the old hotel's bungalow at half the price of the plush new tower. A half-hour stroll from the Metro.

Renaissance Yangtze Shanghai Hotel $$$ *2099 Yan An Xi Lu, tel: 021 6275 0000, fax: 021 6275 0750, <www.renaissancehotels. com>*. Next door to the Sheraton Tai Ping Yang, this Marriott-managed tower competes by offering lower room rates and good dining.

Shanghai Marriott Hotel Hongqiao $$$$ *2270 Hongqiao Lu, tel: 021 6237 6000, fax: 021 6237 6222, <www.marriott.com>*. A five-star modern hotel near the old Hongqiao airport, with large guest rooms and hi-tech communications, the Marriott requires a long taxi ride to central Shanghai.

Sheraton Grand Tai Ping Yang $$$$ *15 Zunyi Nan Lu, tel: 021 6275 8888, fax: 021 6275 5420, <www.sheratongrand-shanghai. com>*. Recently renovated and redecorated, the Sheraton Grand is the top hotel in this part of town. It has an excellent staff, plush rooms and a sumptuous deli.

HONGKOU (NORTH SHANGHAI)

Holiday Inn Downtown Shanghai $$ *585 Heng Feng Lu, tel: 021 6353 8008, fax: 021 6354 3019, <www.holiday-inn.com>*. A block from the Shanghai Railway Station and a Metro entrance, each of the hotel's towers offers four-star facilities; very clean, compact modern rooms; and fairly efficient service at economical rates, particularly through its internet site.

Panorama Hotel $$$ *53 Huangpu Lu, tel: 021 5393 0008, fax: 021 5393 0009, <www.accorhotels.com>*. Affiliated with Accor, this new four-star giant has superb views of the riverfront and Bund, plenty of luxury amenities and excellent room rates, but it requires a long stroll or a taxi ride to reach restaurants, shopping and tourist sights.

Pujiang Hotel $$ *15 Huangpu Lu, tel: 021 6324 6388, fax: 021 6324 3179, <www.pujianghotel.com>*. A backpackers' mecca, the Pujiang is packed with history, from its creation in 1860 to its transformation in 1910 as the Astor House, favourite of President Grant (room 410), Scott Joplin (room 404), Bertrand Russell (room 310) and Albert Einstein (room 304). Modern renovations since 2003 have restored these celebrity rooms and modernised many of the doubles.

PUDONG (EAST SHANGHAI)

Grand Hyatt Shanghai $$$$$ *88 Shi Ji Da Dao, tel: 021 5049 1234, fax: 021 5049 1111, <www.shanghai.grand.hyatt.com>*. As the highest hotel in the world (floors 53–87, Jinmao Building), the Grand Hyatt has lived up to its lofty billing with hi-tech curving rooms, walls of glass, a labyrinth of speedy elevators and restaurants, amenities and services that rank among the best in Asia.

Holiday Inn Pudong $$$$ *899 Dong Fang Lu, tel: 021 5830 6666, fax: 021 5830 5555, <www.holiday-inn.com>.* Next door to the more expensive St Regis and favoured by many Western business travellers, the Holiday Inn comes with clean, modern rooms; king-size beds and many of the services of a five-star hotel. Not in a sightseeing neighbourhood, but it is near a Metro station.

Hotel Inter-Continental $$$$$ *777 Zhang Yang Lu, tel: 021 5831 8888, fax: 021 5831 7777, <www.intercontinental.com>.* Renovated in 2002, this contemporary tower in central Pudong has spacious rooms and deluxe amenities. It also offers tee-times at the members-only Tomson Golf Course that is the nearest links to a major hotel in Shanghai.

Novotel Atlantis $$$$ *728 Pudong Da Dao, tel: 021 5036 6666, fax: 021 5036 6677, <www.accorhotels.com>.* A jazzy hotel with French flair and an internet café in the lobby, Novotel is too far east to walk to the Metro or Pudong's main sights, but it has a quick shuttle to the airport, a children's club and an executive-level 'Ladies Floor'.

Pudong Shangri-La $$$$$ *33 Fucheng Lu, tel: 021 6882 8888, fax: 021 6882 6688, <www.shangri-la.com>.* Shanghai's version of the Asian-based Shangri-La chain lives up to its name with top-flight international services and superb views of the Bund across the river. The new Tower II annexe (2005), with the most spacious rooms in town, makes this Asia's largest luxury hotel.

St Regis Shanghai $$$$$ *889 Dong Fang Lu, tel: 021 5050 4567, fax: 021 6875 6789, <www.stregis.com>.* With extremely large rooms, lavish amenities and 24-hour butler service, this top-end representative of the Starwood line pampers guests as no other hotel in Shanghai can. Located deep in Pudong's south central business district, it requires a taxi or Metro ride (with a nearby Metro station) for sightseeing.

Recommended Restaurants

Shanghai has restaurants to appeal to every palate, led by those featuring its own Shanghai cuisine. Other regional Chinese cuisines, particularly Cantonese, and Asian flavours, especially Thai, are also amply represented. Western dining is making its mark, spearheaded by fine Italian and French restaurants in major hotels, the French Concession, Xintiandi and recently along the Bund, where international chefs are causing a stir with pricey East/West fusions. Restored mansions and villas now house some of the city's most notable eating venues, and everyday fare catering to the foreign traveller is provided by cafés, bars and international fast-food outlets. Exotic settings, as well as exotic menus, make Shanghai an unforgettable dining experience.

Restaurants listed here are arranged alphabetically by location. Price ranges, given as guides only, are based on an evening meal for one, without drinks or tips. Set menus often offer the best value and lunch specials the best deals. Advanced reservations are usually required for top restaurants.

$$$$$	over 400 yuan (over $50)
$$$$	280–400 yuan ($35–50)
$$$	160–280 yuan ($20–35)
$$	80–160 yuan ($10–20)
$	under 80 yuan (under $10)

THE BUND (CENTRAL SHANGHAI)

Bonomi Cafe $$ *Room 226, 12 Zhongshan Dong Yi Lu, tel: 021 6329 7506.* On the second floor of a 1923 bank building on the Bund, this Italian café is the place to recharge your batteries with deli fare and espressos.

CJW $$$$ *50th Floor, Bund Centre, 222 Yan An Dong Lu, tel: 021 6339 1777.* Commanding the highest and widest views of

Shanghai from the Bund, CJW is a smart restaurant with an international menu of steaks, salad and sea bass that are well prepared, if uninspired.

Jean-Georges $$$$$ *4th Floor, Three on the Bund, 3 Zhongshan Dong Yi Lu, tel: 021 6321 7733; <www.threeonthebund.com>.* Contemporary French fare with some Chinese touches from chef Jean-Georges Vongerichten awaits its Michelin stars, but this elegant spot, with thousands of international wines in its cellars, is one of the most expensive, highly regarded and heavily booked restaurants, for lunch or dinner, in Shanghai.

Laris $$$$$ *6th Floor, Three on the Bund, 3 Zhongshan Dong Yi Lu, tel: 021 6321 9922; <www.threeonthebund.com>.* An ultra-modern take on fine dining, Laris is presided over by Australian chef David Laris, whose nouveau-cuisine creations can be wildly inventive. The Vault Bar for cocktails and Claws, Wings and Fins for appetisers are both adjacent.

M on the Bund $$$$$ *7th Floor, 20 Guang Dong Lu, tel: 021 6350 9988; <www.m-onthebund.com>.* Since 1999, M has been Shanghai's premier international restaurant with a gourmet Continental menu and panoramic views from its colonial balcony on the Bund. Legendary weekend buffets and the new Glamour Room for cocktails have enhanced its reputation.

New Heights $$$ *7th Floor, Three on the Bund, 3 Zhongshan Dong Yi Lu, tel: 021 6321 0909; <www.threeonthebund.com>.* Far more informal and inexpensive than the other restaurants in this building on the Bund, New Heights has spectacular rooftop views and a bistro menu covering Asian and Western dishes from Thai standards to fish and chips.

Shanghai Uncle $$ *Basement, Bund Centre, 222 Yan An Dong Lu, tel: 021 6339 1977.* Serving the 'new' Shanghai cuisine, Shanghai Uncle is the brainchild of Hong Kong gourmet Li Zhongheng. Dishes use the freshest ingredients and often mix East/West or Chinese/Asian ingredients. There's another reasonably priced Uncle outlet in Pudong's Times Square mall, 8th floor, 500 Zhang Yang Lu.

Whampoa Club $$$$ *5th Floor, Three on the Bund, 3 Zhong-shan Dong Yi Lu, tel: 021 6321 3737; <www.threeonthebund.com>*. In an updated Art-Deco setting, Asian chef Jerome Leung serves up new Shanghainese cuisine, featuring everything from drunken chicken to Australian lobster, along with scores of special teas and even a tableside tea ceremony.

HUANGPU (CENTRAL SHANGHAI)

Gongdelin $$ *445 Nanjing Xi Lu, tel: 021 6327 0218*. Decades old, Shanghai's most famous vegetarian restaurant offers soy and tofu versions of classic Chinese duck, chicken, pork and fish dishes. The atmosphere is institutional, the service indifferent, but the food is tasty and the take-out counter is a fast-food alternative to hamburger and fries.

Kathleen's 5 $$$ *5th Floor, Shanghai Art Museum, 325 Nanjing Xi Lu, tel: 021 6327 2221; <www.kathleens5.com.cn>*. The glass-enclosed dining area atop the neo-classical art museum specialises in fresh, modern American dishes, with an emphasis on Cajun-style seafood.

LUWAN (FRENCH CONCESSION)

Crystal Jade $$ *Lane 123, House 6–7, South Block, Xing Ye Lu, Xintiandi, tel: 021 6385 8752*. Known for its Shanghainese and Cantonese *dim-sum* pastries and handmade noodles, this Singapore-based restaurant delivers excellent, mostly southern Chinese fare for reasonable prices. Reservations required.

La Na Thai $$$ *118 Ruijin Er Lu, Building 4, Ruijin Guest House, tel: 021 6466 4328*. Occupying the second floor of a colonial mansion, La Na is an authentic Thai restaurant with Thai chefs and unobtrusive service. This is an ideal place for a leisurely, romantic dinner.

T8 $$$$ *House 8, Lane 181, North Block, Taicang Lu, Xintiandi, tel: 021 6355 8999.* A chic Continental restaurant, T8 is a favourite among the city's gourmets, who rate its fusion creations among Shanghai's very finest. The Sichuan-style dishes are especially prized.

Ye Shanghai $$$ *House 6, Lane 181, North Block, Taicang Lu, Xintiandi, tel: 021 6311 2323.* Red lanterns and antique furniture give the dining room of Ye Shanghai a colonial air. The menu is spiced with traditional, medium-priced Shanghai dishes such as drunken chicken.

Yin $$ *59 Maoming Nan Lu, Jin Jiang Gourmet Street, tel: 021 5466 5070.* Evoking 1930s Shanghai with its wooden screens and waitresses in *qipao* slit-leg dresses, Yin is a stylish restaurant with a long bar that serves up a wide range of Chinese regional cuisines.

Zao Zi Shu (Vegetarian Life Style) $ *77 Songshan Lu, Shanghai Huanggong Complex, tel: 021 6384 8000.* South off Huaihai Zhong Lu, this modern vegetarian restaurant is lighter on the oil than most, and its tasty vegetable dishes have made it popular among non-meat, non-dairy eaters. No credit cards.

NANSHI (OLD TOWN)

Lu Bo Lang $$ *115 Yuyuan Lu, Yuyuan Bazaar, tel: 021 6328 0602.* Perched on the south shore of the teahouse pond, this three-storey Chinese pavilion has become a tourist magnet after serving a long line of world celebrities from Fidel Castro to Queen Elizabeth. The extensive Chinese menu, sprinkled with Shanghai specialities, is average, and service is sometimes below that level, but the atmosphere is worth the fairly reasonable price.

Nan Xiang Mantou Dian $ *85 Yuyuan Lu, Yuyuan Bazaar, tel: 021 6355 4206.* A three-storey, no frills dumpling emporium on the shoreline between the famous teahouse and Yu Garden, Nan Xiang nearly always has a queue — no surprise, since the steamed pastries *(xiao long bao)* are fresh, tasty and inexpensive.

JINGAN (NORTHWEST SHANGHAI)

Bali Laguna $$ *189 Huashan Lu, Jingan Park, tel: 021 6248 6970.* Overlooking the park's classical-style pond, this quiet Indonesian restaurant couldn't be more romantic, especially from its balcony on a summer night. The food is good, if not superb, and the staff is discreetly attentive.

Bao Luo $$ *271 Fu Min Lu, tel: 021 5403 7239.* Huge, noisy, smoky dining hall with an enormous menu of superb Shanghai specialities, Bao Luo is the place for group dining on some of the best local dishes in town, including crab, river shrimp and barbecued beef. Expect big crowds and plenty of exotic dishes. No credit cards.

Bi Feng Tang $$ *1333 Nanjing Xi Lu, tel: 021 6279 0738.* Cantonese *dim sum* is served alfresco in fishing village-style bamboo huts on the pavement, making Bi Feng Tang a popular fair-weather alternative to Western fast-food outlets and bars. A second branch, open 24 hours, is at 175 Chang Le Lu, near the Jin Jiang Hotel.

Cochinchina $$$ *Block 11, 889 Julu Lu, tel: 021 6445 6797.* Shanghai's premier Vietnamese restaurant, with more than a hint of Shanghai flavours in its dishes, is housed in a large colonial mansion that affords courtyard dining in the summer.

Darling Harbour $$$ *19th Floor, Paramount Hotel, 1728 Nanjing Xi Lu, tel: 021 6248 0418.* Part of a local chain specialising in Sichuan dishes, this outlet serves good, spicy fare. This historic building has been dressed up with an abundance of chandeliers and European antiques.

Element Fresh $ *No. 112, Shanghai Centre, 1376 Nanjng Xi Lu, tel: 021 6279 8682.* The place for fresh salad and other healthy American-style fare, including soups, sandwiches and smoothies, Element Fresh is crowded in the summer. For similar food, quality and price, give nearby Wagas a try, too (Room LG12A, CITIC Square, 1168 Nanjing Xi Lu).

People on the Water $$$ *Basement, Hilton Hotel, 250 Huashan Lu, tel: 021 6248 0000 ext 1830; <www.shanghai.hilton.com>.* The Hilton's newest creation on the dining front offers seafood fresh from nearby Ningbo, its aquariums and counters lined with the catches of the day and an army of expert chefs to prepare each selection. Waitresses are helpful and knowledgeable, the contemporary setting is bright and the seafood dishes (over 100 choices) extraordinary.

Shintori $$$$ *803 Julu Lu, tel: 021 5404 5252.* Stark modernistic setting combined with sushi and sashimi make Shintori the trendiest of Shanghai's Japanese restaurants. The second floor has good views of the busy streets.

XUHUI (SOUTHWEST SHANGHAI)

Paulaner Brauhaus $$$ *150 Fen Yang Lu, tel: 021 6474 5700.* A very German restaurant housed in an expansive 1930s mansion, Paulaner Brauhaus does indeed have its own brewery, courtyard beer garden and authentic sausages and sauerkraut. A well-appointed second outlet recently opened in Xintiandi.

Shanghai Lao Zhan (Old Station) $$ *201 Caoxi Bei Lu, tel: 021 6427 2233.* Housed in a 1920s monastery across from St Ignatius Cathedral and furnished in period antiques, this museum-like restaurant offers above-average Shanghai dishes served by waiters in uniform. The garden contains two historic train carriages, one used by the Empress Dowager, the other by Soong Qing-ling, where guests can also dine.

Simply Thai $$ *5 Dongping Lu, tel: 021 6445 9551.* With courtyard dining behind the cottage dining room in summer, Simply Thai remains Shanghai's most popular Thai restaurant, reasonably priced, with good food and friendly service. There is an equally appealing second location in Xintiandi.

Yuan Yuan $$ *201 Xing Guo Lu, tel: 021 6433 9123.* Yuan Yuan is a highly regarded Shanghai cuisine restaurant housed in an immaculate two-storey house. It attracts well-to-do, casually dressed diners with its pork and rice dishes and seafood at quite reasonable prices.

Zapata's $$ *5 Hengshan Lu, tel: 021 6474 6628.* This nearly authentic Mexican restaurant has an upmarket feel, a lively staff and a zesty menu starting with tacos and margaritas. Dance lessons, buffet specials and DJs make weekly appearances.

CHANGNING (HONGQIAO DEVELOPMENT ZONE)

1221 $$$ *1221 Yan An Xi Lu, tel: 021 6213 6585.* A classy restaurant long favoured by expatriates, 1221 has a menu of fine Cantonese and Shanghai favourites. Expert waiters wielding long-spouted pots keep the cups filled with eight-treasure tea.

Dynasty $$$ *Renaissance Yangtze Shanghai Hotel, 2099 Yan An Xi Lu, tel: 021 6275 0000 ext 2230.* Manned by chefs who regularly cater for visiting heads of state, the Renaissance Hotel's Cantonese restaurant has a formal Hong Kong look and a traditional menu that's strong on seafood and *dim sum*.

PUDONG (EAST SHANGHAI)

On Fifty Six $$$$ *56th floor, Grand Hyatt Hotel, 88 Shi Ji Da Dao, tel: 021 5049 1234 ext 8807; <www.shanghai.grand.hyatt.com>.* This is a collection of fine restaurants on the 56th floor of the Grand Hyatt – the highest hotel in the world. As you'd expect, diners get lofty views of the Bund from the far side of the river. The open kitchens service a Japanese restaurant, a grill room and a modern Italian eatery.

South Beauty $$$ *10th Floor, Super Brand Mall, 168 Lujiazui Lu, tel: 021 5047 1817.* From atop the mall, the views across the river to the Bund can be magnificent from here, and the Cantonese/Sichuan menu adds plenty of spice. The seafood dishes are superb. South Beauty has another elegant branch, west of the French Quarter at 28 Tao Jing Lu.

INDEX